ORTHO **ALL ABOUT**

Garden Pools
& Fountains

Meredith® Books
Des Moines, Iowa

All About Garden Pools & Fountains
Editor: Denny Schrock
Contributing Editor: Nancy T. Engel
Contributing Technical Editor: Michael D. Smith
Contributing Writer: Catriona Tudor Erler
Copy Chief: Terri Fredrickson
Publishing Operations Manager: Karen Schirm
Senior Editor, Asset and Information Manager:
    Phillip Morgan
Edit and Design Production Coordinator: Mary Lee Gavin
Editorial Assistant: Kathleen Stevens
Book Production Managers: Pam Kvitne,
    Marjorie J. Schenkelberg, Rick von Holdt, Mark Weaver
Contributing Copy Editor: Kelly Roberson
Technical Proofreaders: Richard Koogle, Bill Uber
Contributing Proofreaders: Fern Bradley, Stephanie Petersen,
    Missy Peterson
Contributing Designer: Jeff Harrison
Contributing Map Illustrator: Jana Fothergill
Contributing Photo Researcher: Susan Ferguson
Indexer: Ellen Sherron
Other Contributors: Adams Aquatics, Aquascape Designs, Inc., Beckett
    Water Gardening, Kate Carter Frederick, Liquid Landscape Designs,
    Van Ness Water Gardens

**Additional Editorial Contributions from
    Art Rep Services**
Director: Chip Nadeau
Designer: Ik Design
Illustrator: Rick Hanson

Meredith® Books
Executive Director, Editorial: Gregory H. Kayko
Executive Director, Design: Matt Strelecki
Managing Editor: Amy Tincher-Durik
Executive Editor/Group Manager: Benjamin W. Allen
Senior Associate Design Director: Tom Wegner
Marketing Product Manager: Brent Wiersma

Publisher and Editor in Chief: James D. Blume
Editorial Director: Linda Raglan Cunningham
Executive Director, New Business Development:
    Todd M. Davis
Executive Director, Sales: Ken Zagor
Director, Operations: George A. Susral
Director, Production: Douglas M. Johnston
Director, Marketing: Amy Nichols
Business Director: Jim Leonard

Vice President and General Manager: Douglas J. Guendel

Meredith Publishing Group
President: Jack Griffin
Executive Vice President: Bob Mate

Meredith Corporation
Chairman and Chief Executive Officer: William T. Kerr
President and Chief Operating Officer: Stephen M. Lacy

In Memoriam: E.T. Meredith III (1933–2003)

Photographers
Photographers credited may retain copyright © to the listed
photographs. L=Left, R=Right, C=Center, B=Bottom, T=Top

Beckett Water Gardening: 26B; **John Beedle/Garden
Picture Library:** 100L; **Mark Bolton/Garden Picture
Library:** 102C; **Rob Cardillo:** 13TR, 98C, 106R; **R. Todd
Davis:** 38; **Richard Day/Daybreak Imagery:** 14C, 15TR;
Alan & Linda Detrick: 11CL, 104BC, 105L, 15BL, 116C;
Catriona Tudor Erler: 17T, 101TC, 112R; **Derek Fell:** 110C,
112C; **John Glover:** 11CR, 36B, 37TL, 43T, 67TR, 89; **John
Glover/Garden Picture Library:** 100C; **John Glover/
Positive Images:** 101BC; **Jerry Harpur:** 10TR (Julian Elliot,
RSA), 101L (Beth Chatto), 105C; **Lynne Harrison:** 37TR, 60,
101BR, 108L, 109L; **Doug Hetherington:** 52, 53, 77; **Saxon
Holt:** 1, 44, 95T, 103C, 116BR; **Bill Johnson:** 14B, 88BC,
103L, 104R, 114L, 114R, 115TL; **Dency Kane:** 9T, 65, 66T,
106TL, 106BC, 107L, 115C; **Lynne Karlin:** 66B; **Rosemary
Kautzky:** 13TL, 14T, 17C (R.B. Blitch), 36T, 41TL, 47T, 55,
58, 67T, 72, 86, 95B, 96, 104L, 106TC, 107R, 108C, 113C;
Andrew Lawson: 9B (Simon Shire), 12T, 59B; **Janet
Loughrey:** 4-5, 102L, 102R; **Hanson Man:** 88T, 88TC, 88B;
Marilynn McAra: 110R; **Clive Nichols:** 9BC (James van
Sweden), 75 (M. Upward/R. Mercer); **Jerry Pavia:** 13RC, 33B,
42T, 82T, 99C, 99R, 108R; **Ann Reilly/Positive Images:**
104TC; **Howard Rice/Garden Picture Library:** 15B, 112L,
113R; **Alec Scaresbrook/Garden Picture Library:** 116TR;
J. S. Sira/Garden Picture Library: 98R, 100R, 115R; **Albert
Squillace/Positive Images:** 116L; **Ron Sutherland/Garden
Picture Library:** 99L; **Michael Thompson:** 13RBC, 17B,
41B, 43C, 48, 67BR, 73, 91, 92, 105R, 106BL, 107C, 113L,
114C; **Bert Wiklund:** 111R; **Justyn Willsmore:** 47B, 101TR,
110L; **Steven Wooster/Garden Picture Library:** 98L, 103R;
Alex Zatschkovitsch/Flora Graphics: 109R, 111L, 111C

Cover photograph: Saxon Holt

All of us at Meredith® Books are dedicated to providing
you with the information and ideas you need to enhance
your home and garden. We welcome your comments and
suggestions about this book. Write to us at:
    Meredith Corporation
    Meredith Gardening Books
    1716 Locust St.
    Des Moines, IA 50309–3023

If you would like more information on other Ortho
products, call 800/225-2883 or visit us at: www.ortho.com

Note to the Readers: Due to differing conditions, tools,
and individual skills, Meredith Corporation assumes no
responsibility for any damages, injuries suffered, or losses
incurred as a result of following the information published
in this book. Before beginning any project, review the
instructions carefully, and if any doubts or questions
remain, consult local experts or authorities. Because codes
and regulations vary greatly, you always should check with
authorities to ensure that your project complies with all
applicable local codes and regulations. Always read and
observe all of the safety precautions provided by
manufacturers of any tools, equipment, or supplies,
and follow all accepted safety procedures.

Contents

PLANNING YOUR GARDEN POOL

The sparkle of a stream, the splashing of a fountain, the glimpse of golden fish, the delicate petals of a water lily—all these and more are reasons to add water to your landscape.

A water feature can be as simple as a wooden tub or as elaborate as a stream with bridges, waterfalls, and pools of exotic plants and fish. It can be a formal tiered fountain centered in a patio, or a pool so natural your guests will assume it's always been there. And most water features—no matter which type you choose—are terrific do-it-yourself projects.

Throughout history, people have incorporated the soothing sounds and sight of water features into their landscapes. Water gardens were favorites of the Moors, for whom water was a symbol of life and purity. They positioned cooling fountains in the middle of their formal courtyards to signify the primacy of water. Early Asians, too, valued water gardens as an aid to meditation and delighted in breeding rare fish. In ancient times, Chinese nobility spent their afternoons lolling in small boats on water gardens while servants floated tea-filled cups to them on lily pads.

▼ **The water garden of your dreams may be easier to achieve than you think. It takes planning and effort, but the end result will transform your backyard landscape into a tranquil oasis.**

For Italians during the Renaissance, water was a toy. They loved elaborate fountains and whimsical sprays—some designed to squirt unsuspecting passersby—and installed them throughout their estates. The lavish water features of Versailles inspired nobility all over Europe to build their own water gardens and fountains during later centuries. And well-to-do 19th-century Americans copied and expanded upon the European water features. The fountains at Longwood Gardens near Philadelphia still enchant visitors.

Water gardens have once again grown popular, even in our small yards. Like the water gardeners before them, modern homeowners find that water features are beautiful and peaceful additions to any landscape. But, unlike their predecessors, today's gardeners have better tools and materials with which to build their pools. Flexible and preformed liner materials, for example, have revolutionized design and scaled down installation. Water gardening is easier than ever, and even if you're a novice at growing plants in water, building a garden pond is limited less by your wallet than it is by your imagination.

FEASIBILITY FIRST

HINT

If you want your first water garden to be a large one, consider consulting a landscape architect or water garden specialist to help you design it and to estimate how much of its installation you can accomplish by yourself. You'll save money in the long run by avoiding costly mistakes.

What is feasible?

This should be your first question; to find out which water feature best suits you, your resources, and your space, you'll need to educate yourself. Be a know-it-all before you start and you will be well-prepared to begin your water garden.

Start by reading this book from cover to cover. It contains a wealth of information on everything from principles of design to pumps and plants. Browse through water garden catalogs too. Check out prices and calculate what you can afford. Call water garden suppliers and ask questions about their products. If possible, visit local water gardens. Talk with the owners or with those who maintain them. Visit local clubs—many communities have organizations that sponsor tours of water gardens. If you're well-informed, you'll make better plans, find installation easier, and prevent frustrations down the road.

Size and site

First check out your site. A large water garden with a spectacular waterfall will overwhelm a small lot. It also might tax your budget, your time, and your back. A small garden pool, on the other hand, could get lost in an expansive landscape.

A water garden can enhance any spot—outdoors or indoors—from the yard to the patio, a balcony, or a porch. But some water features are better suited than others to certain sites (and to certain gardeners, for that matter).

▲ **When tackling a large project such as this one, be prepared for the cost, time, and skill it requires.**

THE COSTS

Note: Prices are approximate and will vary depending on the quality of materials and the region. Many suppliers sell water garden kits, which include everything you need from liners to plants and fish. These kits are often more economical than buying individual components. See the Garden Pool Resources on page 119 for a complete list of water garden suppliers.

- Mid-quality flexible liner: $1 per square foot
- Mid-quality pump for a small pool: $80–$200
- Fountainhead: $10–$55

- 7×5-foot kidney-shaped preformed plastic liner: $88
- 6×4-foot kidney-shaped preformed fiberglass liner: $415
- Plants for a 6×11-foot pond: $162
- Biofilter: $54–$1,799
- Professionally installed GFI electrical source: $200–$250
- Tub garden with small fountain: $35 without container
- Small pond kit for 6-foot by 11-foot pond: $885 complete
- Pond kit for medium pond with EPDM liner: $148
- Pond kit for 42-gallon pool with preformed liner: $124
- Waterfall kit: $245

If you're planning anything more involved than a premade fountain or container water garden, you'll also need to check with town or county offices to find out if there are any ordinances that apply to the installation of water gardens. Depending on the depth, you may need to fence it (some cities require a 6-foot fence for anything deeper than 18 inches). You may need to install the water feature at a specified distance from property lines, especially if it's aboveground. Check to see if there are limitations on size, height, and lighting for water features. Remember that both plumbing and electrical work will need to meet local codes.

Be calculating

Figure all costs in advance. Small gardens are inexpensive, but large gardens can cost thousands of dollars. You don't want to find yourself in the position of the would-be water gardener who dug a large hole one spring weekend only to fill it in again because the liner was too expensive and didn't fit in the budget.

You may need to contract out a large project (or parts of it) to a professional. Pouring concrete, installing electric lines, bricklaying, and excavation can be extensive (and expensive) and are jobs best left to the pros.

Consider the cost of maintaining your water garden once it is installed. Pumps and filters require regular maintenance. And electricity and water can be expensive.

■ **Assess your time and strength:** A tub garden will take an hour or two to put together, but a large water garden may take weeks to dig and build. It will also require a good back and strong arms and legs. An 18-inch-deep, 6×4-foot hole may not sound like a big job, but it would probably take a middle-aged man of average strength half a day to dig. Soil disposal could take another half day, depending on what you do with it. Ask relatives or friends to help dig, or hire a neighborhood teen for the job. For large projects, you can rent a backhoe. Remember to calculate maintenance time, too. A tub garden with a water lily takes just a few minutes a week. So does a freestanding fountain or wall fountain. Add plants and fish and you add more time. A garden just a few feet across with a few plants and fish will need your attention for an hour or less each week. Larger gardens can demand two or three hours a week.

SHOULD YOU HIRE IT OUT? A SKILLS RANKING

EASY ENOUGH FOR BEGINNERS
■ Sealing and installing a pump in a container
■ Digging a hole a few feet across
■ Laying flagstone or stacking concrete paving blocks
■ Installing narrow widths of flexible or preformed liner
■ Creating a bog garden
■ Working with sand, gravel, and boulders less than 1 foot in diameter

INTERMEDIATE SKILLS
■ Installing a freestanding fountain
■ Building a stream or waterfall
■ Laying a brick patio
■ Laying small amounts of tile
■ Working with medium-sized boulders and rocks 1–3 feet in diameter
■ Building a wood-sided water garden

CHALLENGING
■ Installing a wall fountain
■ Installing a bridge
■ Working with large boulders and rocks more than 3 feet in diameter

FOR PROFESSIONALS (OR HIGHLY SKILLED AMATEURS)
■ Wiring and other electrical work
■ Operating a backhoe
■ Laying brick and concrete block
■ Installing 1-foot or taller stone walls
■ Pouring concrete

▲ The proper building techniques, such as verifying that the excavation is level, make the difference between a well-functioning water feature and one with chronic problems.

WHICH STYLE FOR YOU?

▲ **This pool fits beautifully into the landscape and is obviously the result of careful planning.**

Water features are as individual as the gardeners who create them. Ask yourself the following questions to help you decide which is best for you.

What size?

■ Do I have an hour or two (or more) each week to devote to water gardening?
■ Is my landscape fairly large?
■ Have I installed a water garden before?
■ Am I an experienced do-it-yourselfer?
■ Do I have friends or family who are willing and able to help?
■ Is there enough money in my budget to spend several hundred dollars or more on a water feature?
If you answered "no" to most of the questions, you should build a small pond.

Formal or informal?

■ Do I like straight lines and symmetry?
■ Does my landscape already have a number of formal elements?
■ Do I thrive on order?
■ Is my lot a geometric shape?
■ Do the doors and windows of my house look out on a landscape designed in grids?
■ Is my home interior formal?

■ Do I find some informal gardens disorderly and messy?
If you answered "yes" to most questions, you lean toward a formal garden pool.

Aboveground or inground?

■ Will digging the garden be difficult?
■ Would I like the water garden located near a sitting area, and should the water be at eye-level when I'm seated?
■ Is the water table high in my area?
■ Do I live in a reasonably mild climate?
■ Is the site in a low spot that might flood if the water feature isn't aboveground?
The more "yes" answers, the more an aboveground pool is appropriate for your site; the more "no" answers, the more an inground pool is the better choice.

Which features?

■ Do I want the sound of splashing water?
■ Will I keep fish in the water garden?
■ Do I want to see moving water or watch it course through my landscape?
■ Are winds at the site calm enough to avoid potentially disturbing a high waterfall or fountain?
If you answered "yes" to most questions, include a fountain, stream, or waterfall in your plans.

Do I want plants?

■ Will the garden receive four or more hours of sunlight?
■ Am I interested in tending new plants?
■ Do I want fish?
■ Am I concerned about keeping the water clear without chemicals?
■ Am I willing to spend extra time taking care of plants?
If you answered "yes" to most questions, add plants to your pond.

Should I have fish in my garden?

■ Do I live in a mild climate; if not, am I willing to overwinter the fish indoors?
■ Am I willing to provide the extra weekly care that fish require?
■ Do I want to minimize mosquitoes? (Mosquitoes can spread West Nile virus).
■ Is having a complete, self-regulating ecosystem important to me?
If you answered "yes" to most questions, add fish to your pond.

FORMAL VS. INFORMAL

Garden styles can be categorized as formal or informal, and water gardens are no exception.

Formal gardens are symmetrical and fit into landscapes designed in grids. They tend to be straight-lined and angular and lend themselves especially well to traditional homes and formal urban landscapes. Their well-ordered appearance is enhanced with rectangular or square materials—brick, cut stone, marble, and ceramic tile. Most wall fountains and freestanding fountains are formal, although as water features become increasingly popular, more informal fountains are available.

Informal gardens are the opposite of formal gardens. They often have an abstract shape and are set casually or asymmetrically into country gardens and medium-sized yards. Because of their naturalistic look, it's critical that they blend into the surrounding landscape as a part of beds, borders, decks, or at the edge of woodlands. Informal water garden materials tend to be round or irregular—flagstone, wood, boulders, rock, and gravel.

◄ Formal pools feature symmetrical shapes and right angles. The bricks reinforce the style while helping to anchor the pool into the surrounding paths.

◄ This informal water feature, with curved edges, is a natural for a wooded lot and a casual, nature-oriented lifestyle.

INGROUND VS. ABOVEGROUND

Inground pools are good projects for beginning water gardeners because their installation generally doesn't require special skills. Aside from digging and hauling soil away, building one is simple—dig it, line it, and fill it. Even when small, they are attractive and fit into both naturalistic and formal landscapes.

Aboveground pools have advantages, too; however, their installation is not without effort. They're excellent for areas where you want the water close to eye level or situated at just the right height for dangling fingers. Aboveground pools are ideal for those difficult-to-dig locations in clay, compacted soil, or among tree roots. They are suited to mild climates where water doesn't freeze and where footings can be set less thick and deep.

Although some aboveground pools require little digging (others, none at all), you still have to build the pool's sides and, depending on the style you choose, this can take masonry skill. The sides can be built from almost any material: brick, stone, concrete, tile, wood, even flower-border edging purchased at a garden center.

◄ Inground pools are easy to build and don't require special skills. They are good projects for beginners.

◄ Aboveground pools require more effort. But, they are well suited to difficult-to-dig locations in clay or among tree roots.

WHICH STYLE FOR YOU? *(continued)*

No matter how small or how large, all water features add a special element to a garden. But how do you go about adding that splash, sparkle, and movement? Think creatively. Take a cue from the water features on this page; they incorporate interesting objects—sculpture, urns, and furniture—and fit the overall feeling of the landscape in which they appear. Consider converting watertight containers into self-contained fountains, or come up with your own original shape or design. After all, a water garden reflects more than the sky above—it also reflects your personality.

▶ This circular pool is a pleasant addition to the terraced seating area above it. The spitter frog fountain tucked under the bold foliage of *Monstera*, adds a touch of whimsy to the otherwise formal setting.

◀ This portable container fountain makes a magical centerpiece for a tabletop, or it can be used to bring the tranquil motion of water to a deck or patio.

▶ A freestanding statuary fountain is a dramatic focal point at the end of a garden path. The splashing water invites visitors from other parts of the garden to come take a closer look.

◀ Decks, either new or existing, can be the perfect spot for garden pools. This deck brings a formal, modernistic note to an otherwise informal landscape.

◀ Water gardens don't get much smaller—or more charming—than this. A tiny, shallow pool has been tucked cleverly into a flower bed.

▶ An organic-looking waterfall in the shape of a gunnera leaf adds elegance to the garden path.

◀ A free-form pool brings the magic of a water garden right up to the house.

▶ This pond is so natural looking, Mother Nature could have designed and built it herself.

◀ Casual decking, plus an abundance of plants, create a backyard oasis.

▶ Tucked into a corner of the garden and paired with an inviting bench, this tiny pool is small on size yet big on relaxation.

POOLS FOR WILDLIFE

No matter what type of feature you install, it will attract wildlife. Birds will take a sip of water from even a simple tub, and they'll bathe in a splashing fountain. Butterflies love shallow pools. Insects and other animals, including dragonflies, frogs, and salamanders will be

▲ **Build it and they will come. Water instantly draws an abundance of wildlife to your yard.**

drawn to your water feature and to the plants that accompany it.

Of course, water gardens may also attract visitors you would rather not deal with—raccoons; mosquitoes; birds that love fish; and even the occasional rambunctious, water-loving dog. But all in all, water gardens extend the ecosystem delightfully into your own backyard.

Water gardens in a country setting may attract abundant wildlife, because animals are more plentiful in locations near their natural habitat. However, even a big-city water garden draws birds, butterflies, and other animals.

Wildlife won't know whether your garden is formal or informal, of course. But the more that a water garden resembles a country pond, the greater the number and variety of creatures it will attract because of the greater variety of habitats it offers.

Although the location, style, and size of your garden all contribute somewhat to your success with wildlife, so will having a diversity of depths, rocks, and plants.

Depth

If you're planning a pool that will support fish and plants as well as other wildlife, you'll need to consider constructing it to

A POOL TO ATTRACT WILDLIFE

TREES AND SHRUBS Attract beneficial insects, provide food and cover for wildlife

WILDLIFE-ATTRACTING MARGINAL AND BOG PLANTS Provide food and nectar for a wide variety of animals

ROCK NOOKS AND CRANNIES Give amphibians cool spots in summer and hibernation spots in winter

ROCK BASKING PLACES Attract butterflies to warm themselves

GRASSES Provide cover near water year-round

PEBBLE BEACH Gentle slope lets animals approach water gradually

FLOATING LEAVES Shade water and provide landing pads for insects

FOOD FOR WATERFOWL Includes duckweed and duck potato

contain a variety of depths. Fish need at least 18 inches of water to survive. To overwinter them in areas where the pool freezes, they will need an area on the bottom deeper than 18 inches. Plants also need deeper areas to overwinter. In a climate with winter temperatures of –10° to –20°F, the pond will need to be 24 inches deep. In regions with average minimum temperatures of –30° to –40°F, the pool should have areas that are 30–36 inches deep. Check with your local cooperative extension service to be sure the garden pool you're planning will have depths suitable to your region.

Rocks

Many amphibians, small animals, and birds like gradual approaches to water. An inclined beach of small stones provides a natural entry into the pool for amphibians and birds, and you may want to include one in your plans.

Rocks and stones at the edge of your garden pond are welcome mats for wildlife. Butterflies and small amphibians will bask in the morning sun on low, flat stones. Birds, amphibians, and even butterflies need shallow water so they can sip and bathe without falling in. Place a sloping rock at the water's edge so it is partly underwater and partly on dry land, thus providing a natural-looking ramp to the water. Large stones near the edges serve as perches for water birds. Stones with nooks and crannies, submerged or placed on edge, make shady summer havens for amphibians and protected sites for them to hibernate in winter.

▲ Lily pads shade the water, keeping it cool, and make cozy resting places for frogs and toads.

Plants

Native plants, which offer natural food and shelter to the birds and animals of your region, draw wildlife to your garden pond. Trees and shrubs are especially good because they provide homes for nesting wildlife as well as food and cover.

Perennials and annuals are attractions, too. Their patches of color draw birds and butterflies to feed on seeds and flower nectar. Grasses and sedges, especially evergreen or semievergreen species, provide cover at the water's edge for the better part of the year. Marginal plants also offer cover and food. Plants with floating leaves shade the water and serve as insect landing pads. Those with smaller leaves, like duckweed, are food for ducks and fish. Submerged plants release small amounts of oxygen into the water, which support insect larvae. Bog gardens are ideal for water-loving birds and insects, providing puddles from which butterflies can sip.

PLANTS FOR ATTRACTING WILDLIFE

▲ Cardinal flower

▲ Parrot's feather

▲ Swamp milkweed

▲ Water mint

▲ Water lily flowers

Note: The following plants are perennial unless otherwise noted.

■ **Cardinal flower** *(Lobelia cardinalis)* grows about 3 feet high and shows off bright red flowers in late summer and early fall. A marginal or bog plant, it likes full sun and is a magnet for hummingbirds. Zones 3–8.

■ **Parrot's feather and water milfoil** *(Myriophyllum* spp.*)* are plants that like full to partial sun. Some of the species help oxygenate the water for fish; all provide an excellent area for spawning. Zones 5–10.

■ **Swamp milkweed** *(Asclepias incarnata)* grows about 3 feet high, and its red, pink, or white flowers attract butterflies with nectar. Monarch larvae eat the foliage. It's a full-sun bog plant. Zones 3–9.

■ **Water mint** *(Mentha aquatica)* grows about 1 foot high and bears small, light lavender flowers in mid- to late summer with nectar that is attractive to bees. It spreads rapidly and can be invasive. A marginal, it should be planted no deeper than 3 inches. Zones 4–10.

■ **Water lily** *(Nymphaea* spp.*)* spreads from 1–10 square feet, depending on the variety. Its flowers come in many colors and grow from 1–10 inches across. It prefers full sun and still water and makes a good place for frogs and other small animals to rest. Hardiness depends on the variety, but most hardy water lilies can be grown in Zones 4–10.

Creating an amphibian-friendly garden

Frogs and toads have been slandered through the ages with myths about causing warts. In fact, frogs, toads, and other amphibians are a great asset to the garden, working hours a day for you on insect control. Frogs and toads relish mosquitoes, devour earwigs at a rate of more than a thousand a summer, and nibble on slugs and rodents. They definitely are worth attracting to your garden pool or pond.

All amphibians have four basic requirements for survival: food, water, shelter, and safe places to raise young. Create the right habitat, and the amphibians will come.

■ **Food:** Frogs and toads have adapted their hunting strategies to use human inventions. It's not uncommon for a toad to stake out a light along a garden path. Insects are drawn to the light, and voila! Dinner. Aquatic plants also provide both food and shelter for tadpoles and adults, and lily pads are a favorite froggy platform for sunning.

■ **Water:** A water source is important both for breeding and drinking. You've already got the pond, but make sure there's safe ingress and egress.

■ **Cover:** In addition to the pond, amphibians appreciate densely planted boggy areas. Here they can hide in the foliage, cool off in the mud, and burrow underground. Rock and woodpiles are great shelters for amphibians. You also might try providing a commercially-made toad house or place a broken clay pot on its side.

▲ **Amphibians earn their keep in your pond by eating mosquitoes, earwigs, slugs, and rodents. Frogs and toads take shelter in shallow areas, like the one above.**

▶ **Butterflies will grace your garden if you provide their basic necessities: nectar and water.**

▼ **Joe-Pye weed is a favorite late-summer nectar plant for swallowtail butterfly adults.**

■ **Safe nursery:** If the pond has fish, they'll try to eat tadpoles, so it's important to have small hiding places for the babies that the larger fish can't get into. Having lured these beneficial creatures to your pond garden, you don't want to inadvertently kill them off. Avoid using harmful fertilizers or pesticides in or near the pond.

Luring butterflies

In the natural course of events, you'll find an occasional butterfly in your garden, but with a little thought and care, you can attract them in large numbers, adding to the variety of species that come and to the delight they bring.

To attract butterflies, you need to provide an environment that meets their basic needs. To thrive, butterflies require nectar for energy, water, shelter from the wind (they are so lightweight they get buffeted about in brisk breezes), and sun to warm their wings and orient themselves.

■ **Leave a wild spot:** Despite their beauty and delicacy, butterflies are creatures that are attracted to all sorts of things most people aren't. Ideally butterflies like acres of uncut grass and overgrown weeds where they can lay their eggs. Dead plants, rotting logs, manure, and decaying fruit are all

Given clean water, birds are more likely to flock to your pond to drink and bathe.

pleasing features to butterflies. Many butterfly species are happy with a shallow dish of clean water. Yellow, orange, and white sulfurs; swallowtails; little blues; and red-spotted purples are among those that revel in muddy puddles, from which they derive important minerals as they drink.

Fortunately, it's possible to strike a compromise between an environment that a butterfly would consider a "dream home" and one that you're happy to live with.

The easiest basic way to attract butterflies is to plant a selection of nectar-rich flowers that will lure more butterflies than you otherwise would have. Choose flowers such as sweet alyssum, borage, common heliotrope, lantana, marigold, aster, stock, chives, purple coneflower, coreopsis, daylily, sedum, lilac, swamp milkweed, and snakeroot. Aptly named, butterfly weed (*Asclepias tuberosa*) and butterfly bush (*Buddleja davidii*) are two excellent choices.

Research has shown that butterflies prefer purple flowers, with yellow as the runner up. Monarch butterfly larvae feast on butterfly weed, so be sure to plant enough to withstand some voracious munching.

▶ To attract many different kinds of birds, erect birdhouses of varied sizes and openings.

▼ This decorative net-covered dome protects fish from hungry predators.

Gardening for the birds

In addition to the sheer pleasure that birds provide humans who enjoy bird-watching, birds play an important role in providing a beneficial ecological balance. Insect-eating birds, especially when they are hunting for their young as well as for themselves, are one of the best natural means of keeping insect pests under control in the garden. Even birds that do not typically eat insects as adults feed them to their young because insects provide more nutrition for growth.

The best way to attract birds to your garden is to provide food and water, comfortable nesting spots, and sufficient cover from predators.

■ **Food and water:** Bird feeders attract seed-eating birds such as buntings, doves, and goldfinches, but birds that live on insects or fruit will look for shrubbery. Their seed-eating cousins will be delighted as well because shrubs provide safe places to nest and to hide from predators. Densely branched shrubs, such as forsythia, mock-orange, evergreens, honeysuckle, and lilacs, are particularly appreciated. For the fruit-eaters, choose plants such as pyracantha and barberry that also provide berries.

Like people, different species of birds look for different features in their homes. Purple martins—which are superb for insect control—like to nest in high-rise apartments. Bluebirds like a floor space of about 5×5 inches and a 1½-inch entrance hole. A chickadee, titmouse, or nuthatch needs a 4×4-inch floor space and a 1¼-inch entrance.

Garden Pools for Children

One of the biggest concerns about water gardening is the safety of small children. A toddler can drown in just an inch of water or in a partly filled 5-gallon bucket. No wonder that parents, grandparents, and neighbors are fearful around any kind of water feature.

No water garden can be made absolutely childproof, but there are a number of ways you can make yours safer. Shallow pools, fountains designed for safety, strategically placed boulders, and fencing help children and water gardens to coexist with less worry. But, of course, you should never leave children unattended even around shallow water or the most carefully designed water feature.

Keep in mind that safety is dependent somewhat on age—a garden that is safe for older children may not be safe for toddlers. You may feel confident that a 5-year-old is safe near a half-whiskey-barrel tub garden, but don't expect an 18-month-old to be.

Even 8- and 9-year-olds should be supervised near water gardens that contain 3 feet or more of water. It's a mistake to believe you can create a large pond and train children to stay away from it. The same attractions that draw adults—splashing water, pretty fish, the joy of dangling a hand in cool water—entice the best-behaved children. And even well-trained children have friends or neighbors who will be drawn to your water garden.

Although you should make sure your homeowner's insurance will cover a water garden accident, the best approach is to design the pool so that tragedy doesn't happen in the first place.

▼ **This shallow, stone-filled water feature brings water to the garden and is reasonably safe for young children.**

Fencing

A fence—as long as it surrounds the pool and has a childproof, self-closing and locking gate—allows you to have peace of mind with any kind of water garden that you want. Pretty picket fencing, 6-foot privacy fencing, stucco or adobe walls—all can keep young visitors out of harm's way. However, before building a fence, check your local building codes. Your community may require a certain type of fencing.

◀ **A bubbler fountain in an urn contains no pooling water in which small children could submerge their faces. This is a good option to keep little ones safe near a water garden.**

Depth

You can improve the safety of your water garden by keeping its depth to an inch or less. Consider constructing a shallow reflecting pool, a millstone fountain on a mound of river rock, or a shallow stream. Fill fountains and tub gardens with attractive stones so a child's face cannot be submerged under the water at any point.

HINT

For additional safety, install a floating alarm (designed for swimming pools) in your water feature. The alarm will sound if the water's surface is disturbed.

Height

Fountains can be made relatively safe by building the bottom tiers too high for toddlers to tip into; walls should be at least 2½–3 feet. Similarly, a wall fountain is a less likely hazard if its basin is higher than a toddler's head. Aboveground pools will be similarly safe if you build the sides too tall for small children to climb onto.

Edging

Every garden pool will have an edge of some material. If the edge is made of stone, brick, slate, or concrete, it will get slippery, from water or from algae growth.

Edging around an inground pool creates a path that beckons children to walk around or balance on. It's better to use turf or edging that blends with surrounding materials to make the contours of the pool less inviting as a play area.

Think carefully before building a shallow beach around a pond. It could prevent small children from falling into deeper sections but might actually entice older, unsupervised children into the water.

Placement

The placement of your water garden also will affect its safety. Don't locate it just outside the back door; small children can easily slip out unnoticed and into the water. On the other hand, if you position the pool far away from the house or out of sight, you won't be able to supervise older children near the water.

Consider putting the garden pond in the front yard only if you're absolutely confident neighborhood children won't be attracted to it. Even then, it's advisable to fence it to prevent children from entering. Also, check with your local building-code office first because some communities prohibit front-yard pools.

A water garden by the deck is striking (and an increasingly popular addition), but it could be dangerous in homes where small children live or where they will be frequent visitors. Any deck-side pool should have a railing or fencing surrounding it or the area where it's located.

► The wide, smooth stone edging surrounding this water garden is tempting for kids to walk along. To keep them out of the pool, a decorative metal grate has been installed at water level.

▲ The wall of this aboveground pool is high enough to prevent a toddler from falling in. But, older children can climb it. For safety, build walls at least 2½ feet high to keep toddlers out.

► Water is a natural attraction for young children. For their safety, keep the water shallow and the feature in full view from living areas.

MATERIALS AND SUPPLIES

evolutionary new materials have made it easier than ever to create a perfect water feature for your landscape. Not too long ago, creating any kind of water feature meant you had to hire professionals to form and reinforce a concrete watercourse, then hire other professionals to install complex plumbing and electrical systems. Today there's an entirely new way to create water gardens.

Flexible and preformed liners have replaced the concrete, and now you can install most water features yourself—without professional help—in an unending variety of shapes, sizes, and styles.

Pumps can be installed with little effort, use regular household current, and recirculate the water (there's no more need for special plumbing). Fountains attach easily to their supporting structure. Filters (which once had to be installed out of the

water) are now often built into the pump. With simplified techniques and equipment, it's possible to install a small water feature in just a weekend.

Although the materials have been revolutionized, the basic tools remain the same. A variety of shovels, a spade, pickax, pry bar, wheelbarrow, carpenter's level, garden hose, measuring tape, and a pair of heavy leather work gloves are the basic tools you'll need to complete your garden pool project.

Make sure all tools are in excellent condition, clean, and in good repair before you begin. Sharpen your spade, tighten the wheelbarrow bolts, and inflate the wheelbarrow's tire. The proper materials and supplies, after all, will help you avoid problems, allowing you to easily execute your project and produce professional-looking results.

▼ **Pond-building materials are more varied and easier to find than ever. In the past two decades, the quality of liners, pumps, filters, and supplies has improved dramatically.**

FLEXIBLE LINERS

▲ Flexible liner conforms to your one-of-a-kind creation. Piece it together as you go. Here, underlayment is being positioned in preparation for placing the liner.

One of the most important innovations in garden pond technology is flexible liner. Developed in the 1950s to replace poured concrete and other materials, it allows you to create pools, streams, and waterfalls in just about any shape, length, and style you can imagine.

Flexible liner will help you build water gardens in places not possible before. Line an aboveground brick garden pool, for example, or waterproof a half whiskey barrel. Make an artificial stream with sand, gravel, and stones arranged on the liner. Restore a leaky concrete pond by draining it and laying liner over the damaged concrete.

Flexible liners are made from a variety of materials—polyethylene, polyvinylchloride (PVC), ethylene propylene diene monomer (EPDM), synthetic rubber (butyl rubber)—

HINT

To make sure there are no sharp rocks that might puncture the liner, walk barefoot (carefully) over the bottom of the excavated area.

and they vary greatly in thickness, cost, and quality. Heavier liners will generally be more expensive, more durable, and more puncture- and tear-resistant than lighter weight liners. As a rule, the more you spend, the more the liner will resist the sun's ultraviolet (UV) rays.

UV light is the constant enemy of liner material (especially polyethylene). It breaks down the chemical bonds in the liner, making it brittle and easy to rip. If you're going to build a garden pond with flexible liner, remember to keep the pond filled with water and the liner completely covered so none of it is exposed to damaging UV light.

Most liner comes in black, a color especially suited to garden pools. Black is natural-looking and blends with the algae that tends to cover the liner after a few months (and helps the liner resist UV damage). Black also gives a pool the illusion of greater depth.

Stock sizes for liners start with 5-foot squares and range up to sections of liner 50×100 feet or more. You can join pieces with liner tape or seam sealer made specifically for this purpose to create streams and other large features.

When buying a liner, make sure it is made for use with plants and fish. Liners for other uses (swimming pools or roofs, for example) will be toxic to living things.

Underlayment

All liners require the installation of an underlayment, a cushion layer of material between the liner and the soil that prevents punctures and tears. Sand is a good choice for the pool bottom and other horizontal surfaces, but can't be laid vertically. Newspaper is acceptable, but deteriorates over time. Old carpet (be sure to remove any carpet tacks) and specially made pond underlayment (which resembles sheets of fiberglass insulation) are ideal.

A good underlayment makes the liner extremely puncture resistant and should be used over coarse gravel or sharp rock, for example, or in locations where punctures are likely.

BUYING THE CORRECT AMOUNT OF LINER

- ■ Mark the exact shape of the pond on the ground with lime, paint, string, or flour.
- ■ Measure the maximum length, width, and depth of the proposed water feature.
- ■ To determine how wide the liner should be, multiply the maximum depth by 2 and add the result to the maximum width. Add an

extra 18 inches for minor measurement errors.
- ■ To figure the length of the liner, multiply the maximum depth by 2 and add the result to the maximum length. Add 18 inches.
- ■ Figure in additional liner for islands and attached bog gardens, which require a rise and fall in the pond bottom.

If the liner does tear or puncture, there's no cause for alarm. EPDM liners can be repaired with self-adhesive patches. For PVC, you'll be able to repair it with a patch and solvent cement. However, you'll have to drain the pool first, clean the area, and let it dry so the patch will stick to the liner.

Installing flexible liner

Flexible liner is relatively easy to install. A water gardener can work alone lining a small pool, but spreading flexible liner evenly in a larger project may require several people.

You'll find that flexible liner has one drawback that preformed liners don't have: You won't be able to avoid folds and creases. As you fill the pond, you'll have to neatly tuck the liner—especially if it's made of less-elastic polyethylene or PVC—into uneven places so the weight of the water won't unduly stress it and weaken or tear it. This can be difficult to do, but will be easier if you let the liner warm in the sun for an hour or two before you start work.

◀ Once flexible liner is in place and the pool is partially filled, work the liner into the nooks and crannies of the pond by hand.

COMPARING FLEXIBLE LINER MATERIALS

Liner material	Cost	Advantages	Disadvantages	Comments
Polyethylene	35 cents per square foot and more.	Inexpensive. Most hardware and home supply outlets carry it.	Low-density polyethylene is acceptably durable, but avoid high-density polyethylene. Polyethylene is difficult to repair.	Purchase black, not transparent. Lasts only about two years in a pond. Will last indefinitely, however, when used in a bog garden where it's not exposed to sun.
PVC (polyvinyl chloride)	50 cents per square foot and more.	Moderately durable; sometimes carries a 10-year warranty. Widely available.	PVC for swimming pools and roofs can be toxic to fish and plants. Modern advances have made PVC more flexible in a wide range of temperatures.	20–32-mil thicknesses.
EPDM (ethylene-propylene-diene-monomer)	60 cents per square foot and more.	Very durable; usually carries a 20-year warranty. Stays flexible even in cold weather. Very resistant to UV-light damage.	More expensive.	Look for EPDM-SF, which is not toxic to fish and plants and is available in 45-mil thickness.
Butyl rubber (synthetic rubber)	80 cents per square foot and more.	Very durable, sometimes lasting up to 50 years. Usually carries a 20-year warranty. Is more elastic than PVC and polyethylene. Remains flexible even in cold weather.	Most expensive. Can be difficult to find.	Generally sold in 30- or 60-mil thicknesses.

PREFORMED LINERS

▲ **Preformed liners take much of the guesswork out of digging and lining a pool or pond.**

Preformed liners: many sizes, shapes, and depths

Standard preformed liners also come in a variety of depths; some include shallow ledges for marginal plants and deep zones where fish can overwinter. For large water gardens—those more than 12 feet long—you can purchase preformed liners in sections that you bolt together and seal with marine silicone. Such sectional liners can be hard to find, however, and require considerably more work. It's better to shop around until you find an existing shape that's right for your landscape.

Although you can buy preformed units in different colors, black is usually best for the same reasons it's best for flexible liner: It's neutral and creates the illusion that the pool is deeper than it actually is.

Compared with flexible liners, the installation of rigid units comes with a few caveats. For example, it's essential that the liner is absolutely level and that you backfill nooks and crevices so the liner doesn't collapse under the weight of the water. Also, you have to be careful about using heavy edging, such as stone. Some preformed liner edges are convex and the weight of stone will crush them. Other edges are designed to bear weight (check with the supplier), but they must be fully supported with backfill.

Keep trees or other plants with invasive roots at least 12 feet away from rigid liners.

Easy to install and well suited to small garden ponds, preformed liners (also called rigid liners) come in many ready-made sizes and styles.

Most preformed liners are made of either fiberglass or rigid plastic. Fiberglass is more expensive but lasts longer than rigid plastic. A small 6×3-foot fiberglass liner starts at around $300 (compared with $100 for a rigid-plastic liner); large fiberglass liners can cost $900 or more. Properly installed, a fiberglass liner can last as long as 50 years. Whether fiberglass or plastic, preformed liners are much more durable than flexible liner and are easier to repair if damaged. Rigid units have another distinct advantage over flexible liner—they make aboveground water gardens easier to install. They're ideal in areas where stony soil or tree roots prevent or hinder excavation. You can place them either entirely above ground or install them at any depth. But don't expect them to support themselves. Aboveground ponds will need a structure built around them.

Inground, preformed liners are especially practical for paved areas where the edges can be supported. Rigid liners are available in many shapes, both formal and informal. And if the wide variety of ready-made shapes doesn't suit you, shop around for a manufacturer to custom-make one for you.

> ### HINT
> A minimum of 2 inches of soil mixed with sand backfilled under and around a preformed pond will help prevent winter cracking and splitting.

▶ **Although preformed liners are ideal for formal gardens, they also can be made to look natural. This one is surrounded by stones and has a small stream flowing into it.**

PUMPS

Still water in a garden pool is beautiful in its own right. But moving water is what adds that splash and sparkle to your water garden. For that, you'll need a pump.

Pumps make streams run, fountains spray, ponds drain, and water recirculate so that waterfalls keep falling. Moving water through a water feature once required complicated plumbing. Today, all you need is a pump. Installation is uncomplicated, and pumps take just minutes to assemble.

Submersible or external?

Pumps are available in submersible and external models, and in both, the mechanism is simply a set of whirling blades that pressurize the water and force it into motion.

A WORD ABOUT WATER

All local water supplies contain some form of chemical disinfectant, usually chloramines. Technically, these chemicals will not harm plants, but will harm attendant wildlife, such as snails and frogs. It's best to remove the disinfectants in a new pond, even if you don't plan to stock fish.

Check with your water supplier to see if chloramines are present in your local water. Then take the following steps to remove them.

■ Eliminate chloramines with a chloramine remover. The action of chloramine removers is almost immediate—you can introduce fish into the pool about 20 minutes (long enough to ensure chemical reaction and circulation of the remover throughout the system) after using the chloramine remover.

Follow the recommendations above when stocking new ponds and when refilling the pond with more than 10–20 percent of the water volume.

When topping off the pond (to replace evaporation, for example), you need not treat tap water. However, you do need to follow these steps:

■ Place the hose in a waterfall or at the bottom of the pond. If at the bottom of the pond, cover the end of the hose with a sock to keep fish away from the newly introduced water.
■ Add the water slowly, in a trickle, to avoid shocking the fish and to prevent them from being attracted to the activity of the water bubbles. (Do not use the hose to aerate ponds containing fish.)
■ Replace no more than 10–20 percent of the water at a time; set a timer if necessary.

Submersible pumps are easier to use than external pumps. They sit directly in the water, and, unlike external pumps that you'll have to locate outside the pond, submersibles are inexpensive. They're easy to install, start without priming, and run quietly. They usually include a screen that prevents clogging. Submersible pumps work well for most small fountains, waterfalls, and streams.

Before buying a pump for your garden pool, check its energy efficiency rating. Large water features require more pump capacity, so they consume more energy.

Look for magnetic-driven pumps, which use less energy than direct-driven pumps. (Be forewarned—generally, the most efficient pumps are also more expensive, but they can pay for themselves in energy savings.)

Pump size

The most important aspect when choosing which pump to buy is getting the right size. Equipment manufacturers rate electrical power in amps or watts, but the critical measure of pump power is the number of gallons of water it will pump per hour (gph) to a specific height, called the head.

HINT

Here's an easy way to calculate the volume of your garden pond after you've dug and lined it. Jot down the reading on your water meter. Then fill the garden pond and note the new reading. Most tell you the amount of water used in cubic feet. Multiply the reading in cubic feet by 7.48 to convert it to gallons.

To determine the size of pump you'll need, first calculate the volume of water in the pond (see the box below). As a general rule, choose a pump that can move the total volume of water in an hour. For example, if your pond will hold 500 gallons of water, buy a pump that delivers at least 500 gallons an hour.

If your water garden will include a waterfall or stream, it will need a more powerful pump. Pumps have to work harder to move water up a slope or to the head of the stream. (If you're installing a filter as well, you may need to install a separate pump for it.) Figuring exactly how much more power you'll need is somewhat more complicated. In general, the pump should be able to turn over the total volume of water in an hour.

There's an alternate way to determine pump size for a pond with waterfalls. First, measure the width (in inches) of all spillways. For a light, ¼-inch-deep sheet of water going over the falls, figure 50 gallons per hour for each inch of width. For example, if you have three waterfalls that are each 8 inches wide, you'd need a pump that can move at least 1,200 gallons per hour (400 gallons for each of 3 falls). For a heavier, 1-inch-deep flow, figure 150 gallons per hour per inch of width.

When in doubt, buy a more powerful pump. You can restrict the water flow with the valve (either self-contained or one installed expressly for this purpose). Also, when you are shopping for a pump for a stream or waterfall, make sure its head, or lift, is well above the height you've planned for your falls.

Other considerations

Buy the best quality pump you can afford. Pumps with plastic housings are the least expensive and often the least durable. Aluminum housings will eventually corrode. Brass, bronze, and stainless steel housings last the longest.

Pumps have varying lengths of cord; check to make sure the cord is long enough to go through the pond and plug in well away from the water. The longer the better, especially since some codes specify that the electrical outlet for a water feature must be at least 6 feet away from water. Avoid extension cords if possible (see "Wiring" on page 47). If you have to use one, make sure it's made for outdoor use and is plugged into a ground fault circuit interrupter (GFCI), a device that shuts off an outlet immediately if there is an overload or short.

Some pumps come equipped with prefilters. If you need a filter, you can determine what type to choose by referring to page 30.

Finally, be sure to buy a pump that is designed for use in a water garden. Unlike other types of pumps, those for water gardens sustain continuous, round-the-clock use.

FIGURING THE VOLUME OF FIVE DIFFERENT POOL SHAPES

For all shapes, the dimensions should be in feet. After calculating the area of the pond, multiply the result by the average depth of the pool. Then multiply that result by 7.48 to get volume in gallons.

RECTANGLE OR SQUARE

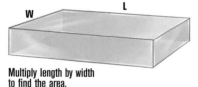

Multiply length by width to find the area.

OVAL

Measure from center to most distant edge, then from center to nearest edge. Multiply the first figure by the second and the result by 3.14 to find the area.

CIRCLE

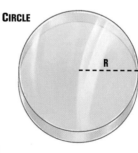

Measure the radius (R—the length in feet from center to the edge). Multiply the radius by itself and then by 3.14 to get the area.

ABSTRACT AND IRREGULAR

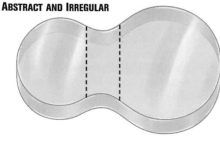

Break abstract and irregular shapes into simpler units (here, two circles and a rectangle), then calculate the area of each. If that doesn't work, multiply the maximum length by the maximum width to find the pool's area.

OBLONG

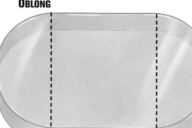

Figure the area by breaking it into a square and two half circles. Calculate the area of the square. Then consider the two half circles as one circle, and calculate its area.

6 QUESTIONS TO HELP YOU DETERMINE WHICH PUMP TO CHOOSE

■ What kind of water feature do you envision? How will you use the pump? How many gph—gallons per hour—will it require?

■ What size is the feature? How much water will flow through the pump? How many gph are needed to operate the feature?

■ What else will the pump do? Will it recirculate water through a filter, over a waterfall, or in a stream?

■ What are the requirements of the filtering system? How many gph does it take to properly operate the filter?

■ Will your feature include fish? If so, how many and what size? A big fish population without aquatic plants may indicate the need for a biological filter. If a biofilter is necessary, determine how many gph are needed to operate it.

■ How many gph are required to operate the type and height of fountain, if you will have a fountain?

◀ The 1-inch outlet in this pump will work well in a moderate-sized pond.

▶ This tabletop fountain pump has an adjustable flow valve.

◀ This dual-purpose pump is used either to minimize flow of water in a fountain or to keep away debris in the bottom of a pond.

◀ This pump will handle 200 to 400 gallons per hour with its small outlet.

HOW TO INTERPRET PUMP CHARACTERISTICS

■ **Model number:** Identify a pump by the manufacturer's model number. It remains the same from dealer to dealer and helps with comparison shopping.

■ **GPH:** Calculate how many gallons per hour (gph) you need, given the horizontal plus vertical distance that recirculating water will flow between the pump and the point where water exits its pipeline. Purchase a pump with a capacity (gph) that's greater than required.

■ **Head (lift):** This is the vertical distance that the pump forces water in the line. Horizontal distance is converted to equivalent head at the rate of 10 feet of horizontal distance to 1 foot of vertical lift.

■ **Maximum head (lift):** At the pump's specified maximum head, it no longer recirculates water. Buy a pump with a head height above the total height of the waterfall.

■ **Amps and watts:** Calculate the amount of electricity needed and the approximate cost of running a specific pump based on your local utility rates. Generally, higher numbers translate to higher electrical usage and higher operating expense. Here's a formula: watts $\times$ 24 hours (in a day) $\times$ 30 days (in a month) $\div$ 1,000 = number of kilowatts per month $\times$ cost per kilowatt = total monthly cost of operating a pump.

▲ Choose from an array of energy-efficient recirculating pumps to power water features and other equipment.

HOW TO ESTIMATE WATERFALL FLOW

Use a ¾-inch diameter garden hose to test what your new waterfall will look like before investing in a pump for it. This test assumes water pressure at the tap measures 40–60 pounds per square inch (normally found in municipal water systems). The hose produces a flow rate of 800–900 gph, assuming no nozzle or other restriction. Let the hose discharge at its maximum rate where you plan to have the water line from the pump discharge water. After observing the effect of this rate on your newly constructed waterfall, decide if you want to keep the flow rate at 800–900 gph or adjust it higher or lower.

TYPICAL FLOW RATES* FOR WATER FEATURES

- **Pond, small:** 40–400 gph.
- **Pond, medium:** 400–1,000 gph.
- **Pond, large:** 1,000–4,000 gph.
- **Fountain:** Varies widely; often 200–400 gph. Check the fountain manufacturer's rating.
- **Splashing statuary, small:** 40–150 gph.
- **Splashing statuary, medium:** 100–400 gph.
- **Splashing statuary, large:** 300–800 gph.
- **Filter, biological:** Recirculates 100 percent of the feature's volume per hour.
- **Filter, mechanical:** Recirculates 100 percent of the feature's water volume per hour.
- **Stream:** Recirculates 50–100 percent of the feature's water volume per hour.
- **Waterfall:** Recirculates 50–100 percent of the feature's water volume; 150 gph per inch of spillway width measured at the fall's discharge height.

*Flow rate (gph or gallons per hour) is an essential indicator of which pump to buy. Determine the pump's gph rate in part by taking into account the horizontal and vertical distance from the pump to the point of discharge. Also consider the pond's volume, which includes water in waterfalls and streams. Check the manufacturer's recommendations for any specific feature.

FOUNTAINHEADS

The most popular use for a pump is to power a fountain, and there are more choices in fountain spray patterns than ever before.

A fountainhead—also called a spray head—is usually sold separately from the pump (although some pumps include them). When choosing a fountainhead, first consider the height and width of its spray pattern, although you can often adjust both with a valve on the pump. Second, choose the style that fits the appearance of your water feature. A bubbler, for example, looks natural in a small, informal water garden tucked into a perennial border or among shrubs. A mushroom or bell is striking in a circular formal pool. And a rotating jet adds dazzle to a modern installation.

Fountains, especially geysers or bubblers, also aerate the water for fish—an added benefit. However, consider the needs of plants. Many, including water lilies, don't like water on their leaves.

Fountains with delicate or tall sprays need some shelter; strong winds distort the pattern, increase evaporation, and deplete the pool of water. Make the pool at least twice as wide as the height of the fountain spray to catch the splashing water.

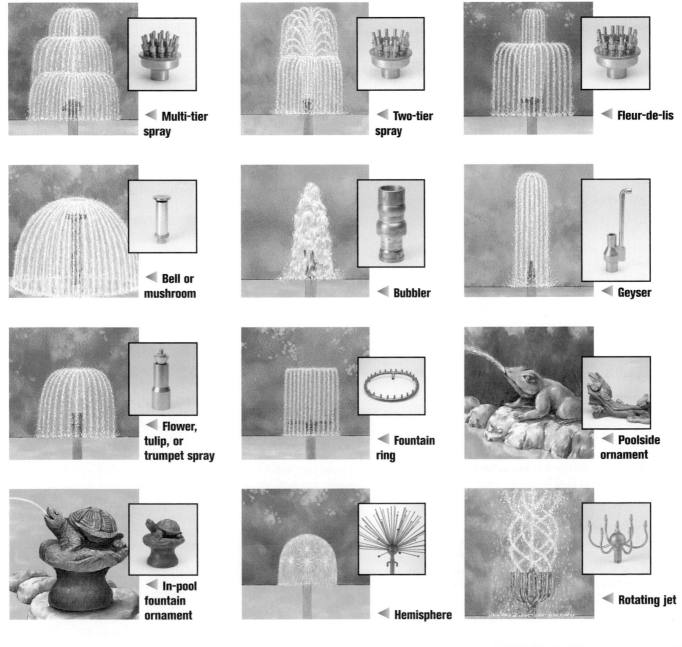

◄ Multi-tier spray

◄ Two-tier spray

◄ Fleur-de-lis

◄ Bell or mushroom

◄ Bubbler

◄ Geyser

◄ Flower, tulip, or trumpet spray

◄ Fountain ring

◄ Poolside ornament

◄ In-pool fountain ornament

◄ Hemisphere

◄ Rotating jet

PIPES, FITTINGS, AND VALVES

HINT

When shopping for plumbing supplies, take along a sketch of your plans so the supplier can help you find the least expensive and most effective setup for you.

Although not as glamorous as colorful water lilies or glittering fish, pipes, and valves and fittings are the workhorses of your garden pond. They're readily available at most hardware stores (or from water garden suppliers), but choose them with care. The right pipes, valves, and fittings can dramatically improve the efficiency of your pump.

Buy smooth-bore pipe (instead of pipe that's ridged inside) to reduce water friction and speed its flow. Plan piping to minimize elbows and sharp bends, which slow water flow.

The following primer will help you choose the right piping and supplies for your garden pond.

Pipes

Pipes deliver water where you want it, and they protect underground electric lines from deterioration or cuts from a wayward spade or other tool. Although copper might seem like the best choice for carrying water, plastic is actually better in garden ponds. Unlike copper and some other metals, plastic isn't toxic to plants and fish. It is easy to cut, simple to assemble, and it won't corrode. Where your plan calls for nonflexible pipe, look for rigid PVC with a schedule-40 pressure rating. For other applications, use flexible corrugated plastic pipe. It bends around corners and other obstacles without using additional fittings. (It won't, however, make sharp 90-degree angles without an elbow.)

In most garden ponds, ½-inch to 1¼-inch pipe and fittings will do the job. If your project requires moving large amounts of water, use 1½- to 2-inch pipe.

Fittings

Fittings are the joints of the water-supply system. They connect the parts, pumps, pipes, and filters. If you want your pump to run both a waterfall and a fountain, for example, you can put a fitting on it to pump just the fountain, just the waterfall, or both at the same time. Other fittings allow you to make the liner watertight where piping passes through it. There are three types of fittings.

■ **Solvent fittings,** also called slip fittings, require a solvent to join them together. They are more complicated to use than other fittings. Use them with rigid PVC pipe. All surfaces need to be clean and dry before applying solvent to the pipe.

■ **Threaded fittings,** those that screw into place, are easy to install, even when wet. Use them primarily with rigid pipes. Make threaded fittings waterproof by winding teflon tape or joint compound around the threads before assembling.

■ **Barbed fittings** (also called push-in or compression fittings) just push together. They're used with most kinds of flexible pipe and need a stainless steel or plastic clamp to keep them secure. They're inexpensive and simple to install.

PIPES

BLACK VINYL TUBING

Clogs and kinks very quickly; best used only where short lengths are needed; black color prevents algae growth.

RIGID PVC

Use schedule-40 pressure-rated pipe and fittings. It is corrosion-resistant, lightweight, and inexpensive. New types are flexible and available in either white or black to make it less visible under water.

CORRUGATED PLASTIC

Extremely flexible, which makes it especially useful for water gardens. Can be expensive and requires barbed fittings with clamps.

BLACK PLASTIC

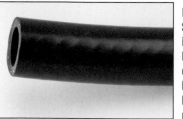

Many brands and styles. Semiflexible, and inexpensive; requires barbed fittings and clamps. Good pipe to bury underground; because it's flexible, requires fewer elbows.

METAL - COPPER OR GALVANIZED STEEL

Is toxic to some pond life, such as snails and dragonfly larvae. Expensive; corrodes. Not recommended.

FITTINGS

REDUCER

Allows you to change from one size pipe to another. Larger pipe moves more water faster because it creates less back pressure and less friction.

T-PIECE

Joins three pieces of pipe. Often used in a pump line to move water to both a waterfall and a fountain.

ELBOW

Changes the direction of a pipe and water flow. Available in 90- and 45-degree turns. To reduce friction, use two 45-degree elbows instead of one 90-degree elbow.

ADAPTER

Joins two different types of pipe or two different fittings, such as a barbed and a threaded fitting.

COUPLING

Joins two pieces of pipe of the same size into one longer piece.

BULKHEAD

Attaches to the side of a water feature. Allows pipe to pass through the liner or wall without leakage.

Valves

Valves control and divert the flow of water. You can use a valve to shut off the water supply, adjust the rate of water flow, split a water source to two or even three separate lines and outlets, or open up a line to drain the garden pool.

VALVES

BALL VALVE

Turns water flow off and on quickly. Not recommended. Valve moves on its own from water pressure.

FLOAT VALVE

Turns water off and on depending on the water level in the water feature. Reduces the chore of adding water during hot, dry, or windy weather.

CHECK OR ONE-WAY VALVE

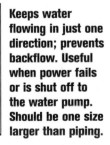

Keeps water flowing in just one direction; prevents backflow. Useful when power fails or is shut off to the water pump. Should be one size larger than piping.

GATE VALVE

Restricts or increases flow. Minor adjustments are easy to make. Can be used as an on-off valve.

TWO-WAY VALVE

Allows you to do several things with the same valve: Shut off the water, control the flow to a fountainhead, or open up a line to drain the pool.

FILTERS

A filter—if you need one—has a big job to do. It will keep water clear and prevent your pumps from clogging with water-garden debris—fish waste, decayed organic matter, floating algae, leftover fish food, and many other unwanted tiny particles.

Not every garden pond that's home to both fish and plants will need a filter, because a well-balanced ecosystem usually "cleans" itself sufficiently. If you can tolerate water that's less than clear, so can the plants and fish. But if the garden pond you are planning will be home to fish and not to plants, you'll have to install a filter to clean up after the fish.

The type of filter or filters—many gardeners use a combination—you'll need depends both on your tolerance for murky water and on the type of water feature you have. A wildlife pond should have a little algae, but water splashing in a white marble fountain must be crystal clear.

After planning the design of your water feature, consult with your water garden supplier to learn which of the following filters is best for your installation.

Types of filters

■ **Mechanical filters:** Using any one of a variety of materials—foam, screens, mesh, or brushes—mechanical filters strain and trap dirt and debris. The simplest form of mechanical filter is a screen on the inlet side of the pump. More complex and larger units are sold separately. Most prefilters (those installed between the water source and the pump to keep larger debris from clogging the pump) are mechanical.

Mechanical filters are reasonably priced, but they clog easily, especially in heavy service, in ponds containing many fish and plants, or in undersized ponds. You'll need to spend at least a few minutes every week (and possibly every day in the summer) cleaning them.

■ **Biological filters:** Biological filters (biofilters) are similar to mechanical filters, but instead of strainers, their filter beds contain live bacteria, which break down toxic ammonia and other harmful substances. In this process, the bacteria convert ammonia compounds first into nitrites, then into nitrates, which plants

▶ **Filters come in all shapes, sizes, and styles. From left: an all-foam prefilter, a prefilter with foam inside a rigid casing, and a biological filter. A UV clarifier is in the foreground.**

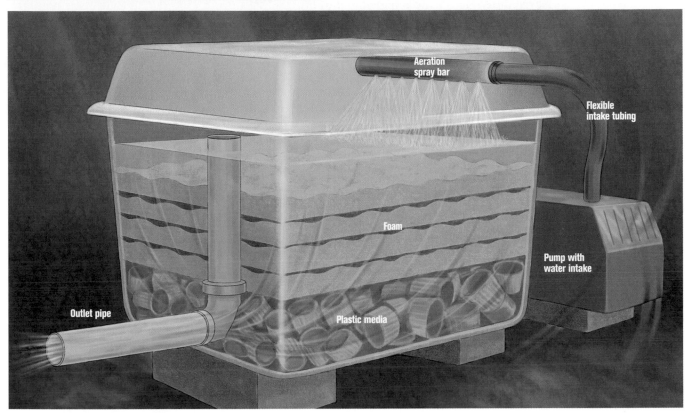

Aeration spray bar

Flexible intake tubing

Foam

Pump with water intake

Outlet pipe

Plastic media

use in their growth. It takes a few weeks in spring for the bacteria colonies to grow large enough to be effective filters.

Clean biological filters every 2-3 weeks by rinsing off the pad or media at the point of water entry into the filter. If you clean any more than that, you'll remove too much bacteria from the elements and end up with a "starter" filter, one requiring several weeks for the bacteria to build back up to effective levels.

In a small pond, you can use an in-pond filter. Large ponds, however, may require unsightly tanks that sit alongside the pond.

■ **Chemical filters:** As the name implies, these filters remove impurities in the water through chemical action. The pond water is circulated through activated carbon or a mineral called zeolite. Chemical filters are often combined with biological filters.

■ **Plant filters:** Using nature's own water purifying abilities, a plant filter is actually a small plant-filled pond or tub connected to the main pond. The plants consume surplus nutrients, reducing algae growth in the main pond. A tub plant filter can be rigged so that water flows into the tub, through the roots, and back to the main pond. Garden ponds with a significant

number of plants won't benefit from a plant filter because the existing plants do the filtering themselves.

■ **UV clarifiers or sterilizers:** The high-tech solution to cloudy water, these are often used as companions to biological and mechanical filters. They consist of an ultraviolet (UV) bulb encased in a clear waterproof casing. When algae, bacteria, viruses, and certain fish parasites are exposed to the UV light, they die. The light also encourages organic particles to clump together, which makes it easier for a mechanical filter to trap them. Clean the glass on the UV light at least once every six months.

Filter size

Pond water is pushed (or pulled) through the filter by your pump, and the size of the filter has to match both the volume of your garden pool and the power of your pump. Before you purchase a filter, calculate the capacity of your water feature (see pages 24 and 26). Then check the specifications for the filter to make sure it can handle the amount of water your pump exchanges in an hour.

HINT

Make your own inexpensive prefilter by placing the pump in a large water lily-planting basket (the kind with an open weave). Fill the basket, covering the pump with pea gravel free of sand.

THE NITROGEN CYCLE

One of the "circles of life" is the nitrogen—or more precisely the nitrification—cycle. It is nature's process of recycling waste, turning poison into nutrients. It happens like this:

In a pond, either in the wild or in your garden, the fish feed on bugs, algae, and other plant material present, and then eliminate in the water. The fish waste falls to the bottom of the pond where it combines with decomposing plant material and turns into ammonia, which is toxic to the fish. Unless the ammonia is properly transformed into beneficial products, your pond will putrefy and die.

Here's where the balance kicks in. Nitrifying bacteria convert ammonia to nitrite. However, the problem still is only half solved; nitrite also is toxic. So a second type of bacteria goes to work, converting nitrite to nitrate, which is a form of fertilizer. In small quantities, nitrate is safe for fish, and as a fertilizer, it feeds the aquatic plants, including algae.

As the plants take up the nitrate, the amount in the water is reduced, thus removing the risk of too-high levels for the fish. The plants grow and flourish, the fish eat the plants, and the cycle begins again.

■ **Beneficial bacteria grow naturally:** Various beneficial bacteria will establish naturally in the water, so you don't have to go shopping for them. However, in situations where your ratio of fish to water is higher than ideal (recommended balance is 15 inches of fish length for every square yard of water surface area) or if you are feeding your fish (thus reducing their need to depend on the local flora and fauna for their meals), then you may need an extra boost in the form of a biofilter to keep the pond healthy.

■ **Biofilters:** A biofilter is designed to provide a nesting ground for the bacteria colony in a pond and to filter out excess rotting plant material and algae. It consists of a container such as a 4×4-foot tank filled with a filtering medium. Possibilities for this material include filter pads, mop heads, and filter rock such as lava. A pump runs the water over the filter material, which catches the solid material, such as plant detritus. It takes 3–6 weeks at temperatures greater than 50°F (less time if you add a bacterial product to the water), but gradually the necessary bacteria will take up residence on the filtering media, and the biofilter will become effective. However, if the biofilter is left unattended, it will clog and cut off oxygen-rich water to the biomedia, killing the bacteria. To prevent that problem, good biofilter management practices and maintenance are essential. Because the beneficial bacteria are aerobic, requiring oxygen to sustain themselves, the biofilter should operate constantly in season. See page 30 for more information on biofilter management.

Creating a naturally balanced pond environment

■ **Patience pays off:** With a little patience, it is possible to create an ecological balance in your pond so that the water stays healthy naturally, thus eliminating the need for filters and their required weekly or even daily cleaning maintenance.

A clean, healthy pond does not necessarily mean the water will be crystal clear. A slightly cloudy, green tinge is normal and healthy. You don't want foul odors or mucky green or brown water. While you may need some chemicals when the pond is new, as the plants grow and the natural ecological balance is established, you should be able to wean the pond of these aids. The process of reaching a healthy equilibrium takes from one to three months, depending on the time of year and region in the country. Factors such

THE NITROGEN CYCLE

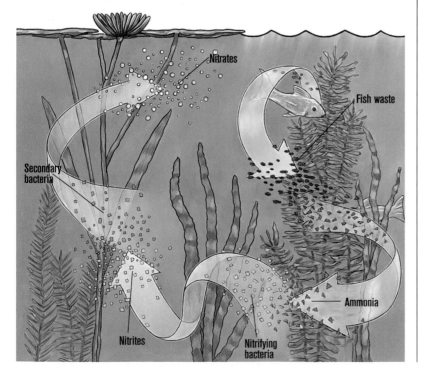

Nitrates

Fish waste

Secondary bacteria

Ammonia

Nitrites

Nitrifying bacteria

as the pond size and depth, amount of sun it gets, water movement, and temperature all affect the pond environment. However, the following combination of plants and fish should provide a stable habitat that requires little or no chemical or filter intervention in ponds with minimal fish. Your pond may occasionally experience a bloom of algae, especially in spring, but as the weather warms, a healthy ecosystem should self-regulate excess algae growth.

■ **Pond elements working in harmony:** For every square yard (9 square feet) of pond surface area, plan on two to five bunches of grasses, one medium to large water lily, five to ten water snails, and two, 4–5-inch fish. Any marginal or bog plants are a bonus. Their root systems naturally purify the water, taking in the pond pollutants as nourishment and releasing oxygen back into the system.

The submerged grasses absorb carbon dioxide as they produce oxygen through photosynthesis. Water lilies shade the water, keeping it cooler, and prevent oxygen from evaporating out of the water. Snails are like vacuum cleaners, eating algae off the plants and pond sides. Fish also dine on algae as well as pests such as aphids, mosquito larvae, and flies. In fact, while it's fun to feed the fish, they do just fine on the natural food available in the pond. Excess food can pollute the water.

Draining and cleaning the pond

If the pond balance has become upset and normal maintenance measures do not bring it back to a healthy condition, then you may need to make a fresh start. It is actually best to rebalance the pond in early spring or late winter just before the growing season starts.

To drain the pond, siphon off the water. Or if you have a submersible pump, disconnect the output piping and replace it with a hose running out of the pond and pump out the water. If you can, direct the nutrient-rich water onto flower beds. Save some of the water in a large tub, and store the fish there until the pond is refilled. When the water is just a few inches deep, check the muck for remaining small fish and small beneficial creatures such as frogs or tadpoles, catch them in a net, and put them in a bucket.

Remove the plants and set them in a shady spot. If you think they'll be out of the water for more than an hour or two,

cover water lilies and submerged plants with trash bags. Store the floaters in a bucket or tub of water.

Bail out the remaining few inches of water, scoop out the muck, and put both on garden beds or the compost heap. A plastic dustpan is a useful tool for scooping up the last of the debris on the bottom. Hose down the empty pond and remove the dirty water. Do not brush or scrub the liner because you may damage it as well as remove beneficial bacteria and algae. Remove the dirty water, add chloramine remover, and refill the pond halfway. Replace the plants (divide overcrowded ones if the timing is right), position the pump, and fill the pond to the top. Follow the same procedures for introducing fish to the water as you do for a newly stocked pond (see page 89).

▲ A mechanical filter with a built-in pump strains particles of dirt and other matter that pass through it and adds oxygen to the water for fish.

▼ Water stays fresh when the elements of pond life are balanced.

BUILDING A GARDEN POOL

Building a garden pond or other water feature is not a difficult task—even for beginners. You can read the instructions presented in this chapter and proceed with confidence, no matter what style water feature you've chosen. If you have a few basic home gardening tools, you're already well-armed for the work ahead, and, with two important exceptions—electrical work and excavation of large projects—you probably won't have to hire an outside contractor.

Electrical work and excavation will be the most daunting parts of the project. Although it's advisable for safety's sake—and may be required by city building code—to hire out most electrical work to a licensed electrician and to contract large-scale excavations, you still need to educate yourself on the basics. Then, you'll be able

▼ Building a water feature is no small job, but it's an excellent do-it-yourself project. Recent innovations in materials for pool and pond construction make the job even easier. You can complete a small project in a weekend, but larger ones will require more time.

to talk more knowledgeably with the contractor if you hire one.

Excavating even a small installation can be a chore—or it can remind you of the days when you were 12 years old and digging a big hole was pure fun. The key to whether it's fun or frustrating lies in correctly estimating how much you can do by yourself. Don't overdo it. For unusually large projects, you might need to contract out the work to someone with a backhoe. (Or you can rent one, if you have the skills to operate it.)

You can use professionals, of course, for other parts of the project if you want (or absolutely have to). However, you'll spend more and miss out on the fun of building your own water feature.

Garden pool installation, like most home improvement projects, is easier to accomplish with two people. Whether you're installing flexible liner, leveling a rigid liner, laying stone, hauling away dirt, or just in need of a second opinion, a companion greatly speeds up the project.

And, as you launch into building your garden pond, allow yourself plenty of time for each step. Most homeowners tend to be overly optimistic with their estimates of the time it will take to complete a project. Remember that there are always unexpected complications, unforeseen trips to the hardware store, and many other time-consuming tasks you won't anticipate.

STARTER GARDENS

Even if you want a big water garden with a waterfall, stream, and a variety of fish and plants, make a starter garden first. A small-scale project offers experience you'll find helpful when tackling larger projects later.

A starter garden brings the beauty of water to your landscape in a minimum of time and for much less cost than it takes to develop a large water feature. It is also more manageable when it comes to time, requiring less than an hour of maintenance every few weeks.

You can have a water garden in not much more space than this book takes up. Sometimes called mini ponds or mini gardens, starter gardens set by an entrance are a delight for visitors. Tucked into a corner of a patio, they're a pleasant source of sound or a sparkling focal point when incorporated into the landscape.

You can make a mini pond that's formal or informal, raised or inground. The logical choice for small yards or patios, mini gardens provide a point of interest in a courtyard or in a tiny plot outside an apartment or condominium.

▲ A container water garden fits beautifully when tucked in a grouping among other container plantings.

◀ Urns are popular containers for fountains. And, they're easy to set up. Simply install a small pump in the bottom of the urn and fill with water.

Homemade or factory-made

Starter gardens can be handmade or come from the factory ready to install. Make one from a ceramic pot. Or try a small kidney-shaped pond formed with flexible liner and tucked into a flowerbed. A premade fountain, filled with fish and plants, or an aboveground preformed garden complete with flagstones stacked in a low wall around a liner can serve as a starter garden. There are even portable water gardens.

Starter gardens are an inspiration. Many people who begin small find they've enjoyed their first creation so much that they want to do a second, more ambitious feature, building on the skills they have acquired. Beginning gardens can also provide the first piece of a much larger project. For example, your small pool could eventually become the foot of a waterfall or a stream. Or, it could be the first in a series of pools connected by bridges or pathways.

▲ Clay pots and pottery shards create a whimsical fountain that takes little time to build or maintain.

Your starter garden could be just a temporary one, there until you move on to bigger projects. If you dispose of it, you can reuse the flexible liner and resite the flagstones and boulders in the landscape. When finished with a water garden container, you can fill it with soil and use it as a planter. And you can reuse a pump in a new water feature or sell it to another aspiring water gardener.

Fish and fountains

For plants and fish, a mini garden should hold at least 5 gallons of water, but eliminate the fountain. A fountain in a container that small splashes too much for fish and plants. Splashing interferes with plant growth and creates currents the fish have to fight. Instead, equip minimum-size gardens with a small poolside spitter fountain or a gentle aquarium bubbler to aerate the water without creating too much disturbance.

▲ A small concrete basin is perfect if you don't have room for a large pond.

HINT
If water becomes cloudy or foul smelling in a small starter water garden, remove ten percent of the water from the bottom with either a siphon hose or water pump. This reduces the buildup of toxic organic wastes.

► A classic bamboo fountain in a large ceramic urn planted with a single water plant creates a tranquil and easy container water garden.

Container water gardens

Container water gardens are perhaps the easiest starter water gardens. You can build a container garden in an hour or two with no digging and little expense. And you can locate them in places you may not have considered for a water garden—places unsuitable for any kind of large-scale pond project, such as on a deck.

oversized dishes or bowls; boulders or rocks with hollows; wooden buckets; iron kettles; claw-foot bathtubs; and even rubber boots. Try using an item you can fully or partially sink into the ground, depending on your location. Inground locations help minimize summer temperature fluctuations. You especially want to sink unattractive plastic containers, such as buckets and dishpans, into the ground up to their lip, then disguise them with plants and stones.

If you're planning to have fish and simply must have an aboveground starter garden, locate it in a spot that receives afternoon shade during the summer.

Is it waterproof?

After choosing your container, check whether it is watertight. Place it on a nonporous, dry surface, such as a sidewalk or driveway, then fill it with water. Let it sit for a day, checking occasionally for leaks. If it leaks, seal minor cracks from the inside with aquarium or silicone sealant.

Make wooden and porous containers watertight by lining them with a flexible liner or painting them with a sealant designed especially for water gardens. (You must seal or line whiskey-barrel halves to keep impurities in the wood from killing fish.) If you're using flexible liner, fold it carefully, tuck it into all the nooks and crannies of the container, and staple or glue the edges to the container with silicone sealer or rubber adhesive that is made specifically for water features.

To include a fountain in a container water garden with no drainage hole, drill a hole in the container. Next, cut a small patch of flexible liner, punch a hole in it, and thread the electrical cord for the pump through it and into the pot. Spread caulk or sealant over the patch, and attach the patch to the container (the caulk acts as an adhesive). After installing the pump, pull excess cord out of the container through the hole in the patch. Caulk around the cord at the patch to tightly seal the pot.

Virtually any kind of container can be used for a water garden. If it holds water—or can be made to hold water—you can turn it into a water garden. Here are some suggestions: whiskey-barrel halves with a liner; galvanized buckets or livestock troughs (older ones that are no longer shiny, otherwise they can be toxic);

▲ **Among the easiest and least expensive of all water features, a container water garden is perfect by an entryway, or anywhere you don't want to excavate.**

Starter features

■ **Plants:** Choose plants for your container in keeping with its scale. Miniature water lilies, fairy moss (*Azolla filiculoides*), dwarf cattail (*Typha minima*), water-loving iris (such as *Iris laevigata*), or corkscrew rush (*Juncus effusus* 'Spiralis') are naturals for growing in container water gardens. Plants that trail over edges such as parrot feather (*Myriophyllum aquaticum*) with its feathery leaves and curling stems, also work well.

■ **Fish:** If you'll be stocking your mini pond, you'll need to balance plant needs for sun with fish needs for oxygen. Most water garden plants do best with six or more hours of full sun. That much sun on a hot day can heat up the water significantly. In turn, the water becomes oxygen-depleted, which stresses the fish. However, you can help fish get enough oxygen even in a warm site by positioning your starter garden where it receives afternoon shade. Keep a min-max thermometer in the water, and never let the water get warmer than 85°F. If fish surface to gasp for air, provide aeration to the water immediately. Use a small battery-powered aeration pump or an air stone, a device connected to a small external pump and placed in the pool.

Because your starter garden will hold only a few fish, you may need to control the population by relocating offspring.

■ **Fountains:** A charming addition to a water garden, a fountain also helps to oxygenate the water. The fountainhead and volume have to be just right, however, in container water gardens. Avoid large, high sprays; choose a spray pattern that is in keeping with the container style. In addition, remember that most floating plants don't like their leaves splashed. If the container is quite small, choose between having fish and plants or just a fountain.

You'll need only the smallest of pumps—a fountain or statuary pump is a good choice—and it should allow you to adjust the fountain spray to the right size for the container garden. Hide the electrical cord among plants, or bury it under gravel.

Winter care

You can leave container water gardens outdoors during the winter in mild climates where average temperatures stay above 20°F. In these mild areas, you can sink the container into the ground, leaving only an inch or two of it visible, and this will sufficiently insulate the container from temperature fluctuations.

In colder climates where average winter temperatures fall to –10°F or below, bring container water gardens—especially ones made from breakable materials such as terra-cotta and ceramic—indoors. Also drain starter water gardens that are installed in the ground, so they don't crack.

CREATING A CONTAINER WATER GARDEN

1. Seal: Any container that you can waterproof can be turned into a water garden. Plug drainage holes with a rubber-gasketed stainless steel bolt or a piece of liner spread with caulk. Seal any minor cracks with caulk or brush on water garden sealant. Use flexible liner to waterproof wooden and other leaky containers.

2. Install the pump: To keep fish and plants, add an aquarium bubbler or small spitter fountain to oxygenate water. To determine pump size, measure the container volume by filling it from 5-gallon buckets. Conceal the cord, and plug it into a GFI outlet.

3. Fill: Fill the container with water to within an inch or so of the top. Before planting or stocking with fish, add a chloramine remover and wait at least 20 minutes (refer to page 23 before beginning this process).

4. Plant: Plants act as natural filters to keep the water clear. Choose plants with a variety of shapes, textures, and colors. Include some that will dangle over the edge and others, such as grasses or sedges, that are tall and spiky. You may need to set the smaller pots on bricks to raise them to the correct depth.

5. Add fish: Fish make an ordinary water garden extraordinary. Allow them to adjust gradually to the water temperature by leaving them in their original water in a plastic bag. Tie the bag and let it float in the container water. After 10 minutes, release the fish. Feed them only occasionally; overfeeding can kill them.

POSITIONING: ENVIRONMENTAL CONSIDERATIONS

Where you place a water feature is almost as important as what type of feature you choose. Position it well and you'll have thriving, healthy fish; plants that bloom and grow happily; clear water; and minimal maintenance. Position it badly and you'll risk diseases of fish and plants, green water, and maintenance problems.

When deciding where to position your water garden, think about the following environmental considerations.

■ **Sun:** If you want plants, pick a site receiving at least four to six hours of direct sunlight daily. Most water plants grow in sunny locations. Avoid sun-baked sites, however. They heat the water, which speeds evaporation and kills fish. You can enliven shady spots with a water feature, turning them into cool havens on hot summer days. However, because few plants thrive in full shade, choose a water feature without plants.

■ **Trees:** As a rule, you should locate your water feature away from tall plants and trees (consider their mature height, not their present height). Tall plants cast too much shade, and trees drop leaves and seeds that can pollute the water (or, like yews and walnuts, can poison it). Tree roots can present excavation problems and damage water garden liners.

■ **Elevation:** Low spots might seem ideal for a water feature, but remember that they collect runoff from lawns and are prone to flooding. Low spots also make a garden

▲ **A small pond with a Japanese deer-scare fountain brings drama to the flagstone patio. It also creates a lovely transition to the landscaped area beyond.**

▼ **Not only is this water garden close to a sitting area for regular enjoyment, it's also in a site sheltered from premature freezing.**

pond hard to drain without a pump and are pockets for frost and early freezes. If you must put your water feature in a low spot, build a berm or install drain pipes to prevent all water from flowing into it.

On the other hand, a sloping site—even one that rises or drops off sharply—is perfect for certain water features. Retaining walls and terraces can serve as the foundation for striking garden-pond designs. Slopes also provide perfect sites for one or a series of waterfalls.

■ **Wind:** Position your garden pond so it's sheltered from the wind. Wind can distort the pattern of a fountain, damage the succulent stems of bog plants, and harm floating plants that need tranquil water. It also speeds the evaporation of water. If wind is an unavoidable problem, consider

▶ If your garden is already shaping up informally with naturalistic plantings, then a pond such as this one would blend in nicely. The rough stone edging and undulating shape make it seem as though it's always been there.

◀ This water feature, while very natural looking, is likely to have maintenance problems from leaves falling into the water.

▼ The gracefully arched bridge is perfectly placed to cast a reflection in the still water underneath it.

erecting a hedge, screen, or fence with gaps, such as trelliswork. (A solid fence can actually increase wind flow by funneling breezes over and down.)

■ **Utility access:** Locate your water feature near a readily available water source. You'll be topping off your pond more often in hot weather and cleaning it out occasionally with spray from a hose. Also, site the pond near an existing outlet if your plan includes electrical features. You can run a line and freestanding GFI outlet to the water feature, but that can be expensive.

■ **Reflection:** One of the delights of water features is that they reflect what's above or next to them, such as open sky or a lovely flower bed. However, if they're positioned near a utility pole or another eyesore, you will simply double an unattractive view.

To see exactly what your water garden will reflect, lay a large mirror on the spot, if possible, to check the reflected view. This will also help you observe the direction and quality of reflected light at different times of the day.

■ **Existing landscape features:** Site your garden pond several feet away from fences, buildings, and other landscape features so you'll have room to maintain it from all sides and so the pond doesn't create moisture problems for buried posts or foundations. You will also need to leave several feet (most local building codes require a 5-foot clearance) between the site and any fences and buildings to prevent construction problems.

■ **Water table:** If you live in an area with a high water table, you'll want to position your water feature on an elevated site.

Rising water tables can push the liner out of the ground, distorting and damaging it. Do a little advance work in the spring. That's when water levels are likely to be the highest. Determine your water level by digging a narrow hole 3 feet deep. Cover it with waterproof plastic—to divert rain—and a piece of thick scrap wood to prevent someone from stepping into the hole. Check it over a two to three week period to see if the water level has risen.

DEALING WITH UTILITY LINES

When planning an inground water feature, call the phone, cable, gas, and electrical companies and ask them to mark buried lines so you can avoid digging in those locations. Or use the national Call Before You Dig Line at 1-800-922-4455. It is extremely dangerous to cut through a utility line with a spade or backhoe, not to mention expensive to restore the damaged lines if you cut off power to your neighborhood.

Locate a garden pond away from utility lines. Don't place an aboveground feature over buried lines.

If utility lines interfere significantly with your plans, your utility company may be willing to move them. Some companies will perform this service at no cost to you.

POSITIONING: DESIGN CONSIDERATIONS

HINT

If your water feature will make splashing sounds, consider where and when you'll hear it. A trickle or splash may sound refreshing during the day but annoy you at night through your bedroom window. You can remedy this annoyance with an automatic timer, wired independently from the pump that recirculates the water.

a patio. Garden ponds are part of the design, not just add-ons.

One way to make a water garden seem like it's always been there is to study the contours of your land. Even seemingly flat sites have slight rises and slopes. Although you don't want to put your water garden in a very low spot, you might want it to hug a curve at the bottom of a slight slope for a natural look.

Sometimes a water garden will fit logically into the lines and contours of your landscape—tucked into a flower bed or set in a just-perfect spot next to a deck.

Garden pools, more than most other landscape elements you will consider, must fit perfectly into the overall layout. After all, a water feature is likely to be one of the highlights of your landscape. Find the best site to get the most out of your pool.

Uses and views

One of the first things to consider when positioning your water feature is how you'll use it. Do you desire something cool and splashing to enjoy while sitting on your patio or deck? Then you'll want the pond close by. Or, maybe you're envisioning a lovely formal pool that will serve as the focal point of the overall landscape. That means you'll be positioning it at a distance so you can view it with the landscape as a whole. Perhaps you want to create a highly naturalistic wildlife habitat. That suggests a location in a less-used part of your property where it won't matter if things get a little wild and overgrown and where humans won't continually scare off animal visitors.

Always integrate a water feature into the landscape. Never just plunk it into the middle of a lawn, isolated from everything else. The most successfully designed water features are usually attached to another part of the landscape—a flower bed, a deck,

▲ **A large pool above serves as a destination at the far reaches of the property. The heavily wooded area surrounding the pool provides food and shelter for birds and animals, and makes the location an ideal wildlife habitat.**

▶ **This whimsical fountain in an aboveground pool takes aim to squirt anyone who leans in too close.**

Elevation and surroundings

Consider, too, from what elevation you'll be viewing the water feature. If you'll be seeing it from some distance, it's ideal to locate it so you look at least slightly down upon it. If the pond will be near a seating area, it's pleasant to have it close to chest level (when seated)—to invite dangling fingers in the cool water or view the fish up close. Locating a water garden so you have to look up to view it is seldom a good idea.

Whenever possible, "borrow" from the neighboring landscape. If you have an especially lovely tree, for example, it makes sense to put the water garden where it can reflect some of the spring or fall color. Or, use your garden pond to underline a pretty view into an adjacent field or mark the entrance into a woods.

When well-designed, water features offer an opportunity to make your landscape feel bigger. Run a rectangular pool with the long side parallel to your main view from the house to make the yard seem longer. A triangular pool with its base pointing to the far end of the yard exaggerates the perspective and makes the landscape appear larger.

Smaller pools also add unexpected interest for visitors who happen upon them. Consider tucking a small pond into a side yard or around the bend of a curving flower bed, suggesting that the landscape is packed with surprises if the visitors keep looking. Include space for a bench or outdoor chairs—a perfect location to enjoy your pond.

▲ **This formal reflecting pool is positioned perfectly to mirror the sky, some large trees, the decorative jar, and the flowering plantings on either side of the pool.**

▶ **People seated on the terrace have a lovely view down into the pool. The steps connect it to the terrace, inviting visitors to come right down to the water's edge.**

▶ **Ponds and pools are ideal for positioning next to a deck or patio where their beauty can be enjoyed up close. This pool brings the water near to those sitting on the bench.**

"Test drive" the position

Wherever you place your water feature, "test drive" its position by marking its outline with a garden hose, rope, garden lime, or white flour. Live with the stand-in for a week or so. This will help you decide if the new position capitalizes on views from the house, patio, and other spots on your property. (View the marked-in garden from every window in your house.) This trial run will also ensure that the water feature fits in with existing traffic patterns in your landscape and leaves enough space for outdoor furniture and other objects. Check, too, how much light the test site gets, and take note of the wind in that area.

DEPTH

The depth of your water garden depends on a number of factors— its size; what fish, wildlife, and plants you will include; and what type of soil you have. Although most garden ponds may look deep, even large water features are often no deeper than 2 feet. That's good news for do-it-yourselfers—and their backs. However, the deeper the pond, the easier it is to stabilize its temperature. Except in the coldest climates, a pond 24 inches deep usually won't freeze solid, a condition that kills fish and damages rigid liners.

Deeper ponds also stay cooler in summer. Small, shallow ponds (less than 18 inches deep) heat up quickly, depleting oxygen and stressing fish and possibly killing them. Shallow water features also are more subject to excess algae growth during hot weather than larger ponds.

Small ponds, those with a surface of five to ten square feet, can be as shallow as 12 inches (18 inches is preferred). Pools of 50 to 500 square feet should be between 18 and 36 inches deep. And, large ponds, those of 500 square feet or more, can be up to 5 feet deep.

To some extent, the depth of your pond may be dictated by soil type. Stony soil or soil with hardpan (a difficult-to-penetrate crust from several to many inches beneath the surface) may limit the depth you can dig. Tree roots may also keep you from making a pond as deep as you'd like. Before finishing your pool plan, dig several holes in the proposed site to the maximum planned depth to check for roots and other conditions that may get in the way of digging.

A pond without animals and plants can be one depth throughout. However, to include fish and plants, the pool should have a variety of depths. Here are the depths each element requires.

■ **Fish:** Although surface area tends to be more important for fish than depth, water depth does play a role. The vast majority of fish thrive in standard depths of 18–24 inches, but koi (because of their large size) do best in water that is at least 36 inches deep. Orfes and goldfish do fine in shallow water as long as the water stays reasonably cool and oxygenated.

Some ponds, especially those in cold areas, need deep zones in which fish can overwinter. In areas where average winter temperatures are from 5°F to –20°F, the pool should have a section that is 24 inches deep to ensure an unfrozen area for fish. If you live in an area where temperatures drop below that, the deep zone should be 36 inches deep. These deep areas are also excellent spots to overwinter less hardy water plants.

■ **Marginal plants:** Marginal plants, such as cattails and pickerel weed, are useful design tools in water gardening. With their feet in the water and their heads in the air and sun, they create a smooth transition from the pool to its borders with the landscape.

▼ **A pond with a variety of depths can support many different plants. Here, shallowly planted marginal and bog plants share the pond with water lilies, which require deep water.**

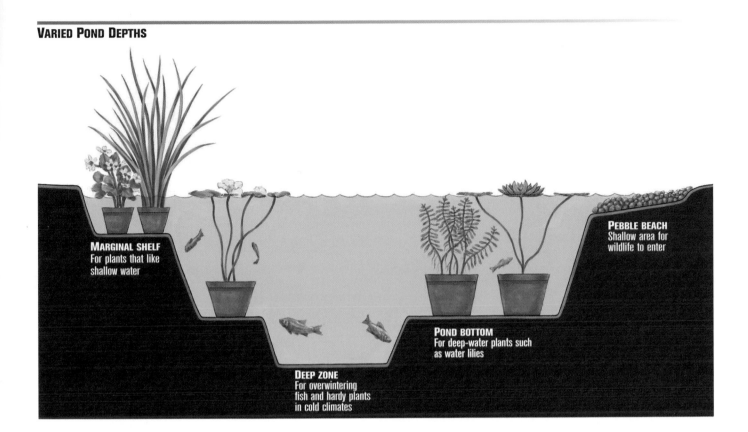

Most marginals rest on a constructed shelf 8–12 inches deep. While each plant has different depth requirements, nearly all do well with their crowns either level with the water surface or as much as 2 inches beneath it. When calculating the depth for the marginal shelf, remember to include the pot and plant size. Tall plants, for example, will need fairly wide and deep containers but their crowns still need to be near the water surface.

■ **Submerged plants:** Although some of these plants are completely submerged, others will occasionally thrust flower spikes above the water surface. Planted in pots or baskets on the bottom of the pond, most of them should be placed deep enough to reach their mature height without surfacing. The depth for each plant differs. Many require water 18–24 inches deep; others do fine in just a few inches of water. When deciding the depth of your pond, do a little research on submerged plants to make sure your favorites won't be too tall for your planned water garden.

■ **Waterlilies and other deep-water plants:** Many plants for garden pools, including water lilies, grow from roots anchored in pots in the lower parts of the pond; they send up leaves that float on the surface of the water. Plant the smallest of these varieties, such as miniature water lilies, in water as shallow as 6 inches. You can also place them among the plants on the shelf for marginals. Provide the others with water that's 12–24 inches deep. Place them on the bottom of the pond. Some floaters have a substantial spread, so if you're planning to grow several, make sure there's room for all.

■ **Wildlife:** Small amphibians, birds, and many other animals appreciate a gentle surface at the edge of the pond, usually in the form of a pebble beach. Make the beach 4–6 inches deep at its deepest point, with a lip at the submerged end to prevent the pebbles from washing into the deeper part of the pond. You can also mortar a row of stones along the edge to prevent them from washing in.

The entire stretch from shore to drop-off, (including the underwater portion) should be at least 2–3 feet long, with one-third of that submerged. Underlay the entire beach surface with flexible liner, and use washed sand, pea gravel, pebbles, or all three for the beach itself. (Avoid sharp sand or stone that might damage the liner.)

Keep in mind that pebble beaches have a drawback; they are prone to filamentous algae unless you provide adequate water circulation. If you're not diligent in pulling it out, you'll have to tolerate algae growth.

HINT

Get a plant at just the right depth with the help of stacked bricks or plastic storage crates filled with rocks and tied together with wire. Concrete blocks, if properly cured, also work well.

ELECTRICAL WORK

HINT

When designing your water feature, consider installing a separate switch inside the house. You'll be able to turn on fountains and lights with the touch of a finger without going outside.

Although you can have a delightful garden pool without electricity, power is what creates that splash from a fountain, ensures water clarity with a filter, sparks dazzling effects with lights, and warms the pond with a heater in winter.

While nearly all elements of a modest-size water garden are do-it-yourself projects, the electrical work is one area that most homeowners should leave to professionals. Only those who have extensive experience in electrical work should attempt to wire a water feature themselves. Even then, some municipal codes require that a professional do the work.

Codes

Before you finish planning your water feature, check codes in your area to see whether professional installation is required, how far the water feature must be from the electrical outlet, and whether electrical lines must be buried (and how). And, even if you hire a professional, familiarize yourself with the electrical requirements of your garden pool. You'll do better planning and will be able to discuss the project knowledgeably with the electrician, having all the necessary information that person needs.

Circuits

The most important step in ensuring a safe water feature is running it on a GFI (sometimes called GFCI), a ground-fault circuit interrupter. You've probably seen them in bathrooms—they're the ones with a red test light or button. These circuits are very sensitive and automatically shut off if they're sliced through or come in contact with moisture (or with you). If a GFI isn't near your water feature, you must have one installed, which costs $200–$250 when done by an electrician.

The closer the water feature is to the electrical outlet, the more economical the wiring of the project will be. Extending lines out into the garden costs more, and after a distance of 100 feet, voltage begins to drop slightly.

Water garden accessories can be run on three different voltages: 120 volt, 240 volt, and 12 volt. You can use your home's existing 120-volt electrical system to power most pumps, filters, lights, and other pond accessories. The disadvantage of using a 120-volt system is that you may need to bury the cable in protective piping as well as get a permit to do the work.

WATER GARDEN ELECTRICAL SET-UP

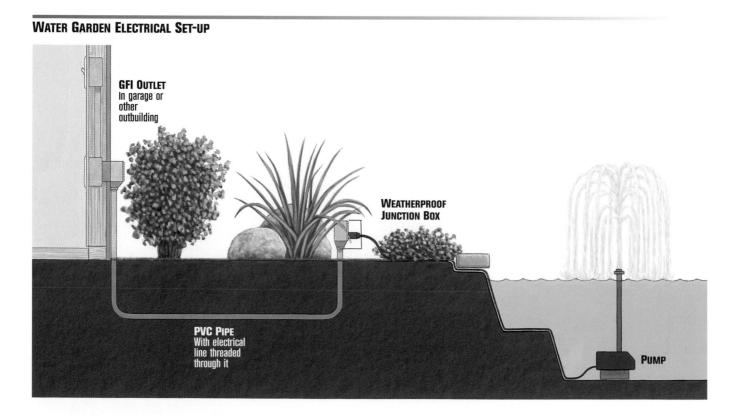

GFI OUTLET
In garage or other outbuilding

WEATHERPROOF JUNCTION BOX

PVC PIPE
With electrical line threaded through it

PUMP

If your electrical needs will be substantial, consider installing 240-volt service, especially if the pond will have a heavy-duty recirculating pump and fountains (check your pump requirements). This service can carry more power and must be installed by professional electricians.

An alternative lighting power source is a low-voltage system. These 12-volt systems present less danger of shock, so the cable can lay on top of the ground or be buried only an inch or so beneath the soil. Installing them usually doesn't require an electrician or a permit. They extend from a plug-in transformer, which reduces regular household current to 12 volts, and you can install them in about an hour.

■ **Outlets:** Small pumps and accessories plug into 120-volt outlets. However, it's safest if the outlet is four to six feet from the water. Some local ordinances require that the outlet is that far away.

For large pumps, 15–20 amps or greater, you'll need to wire the cord directly into the circuit with the connection enclosed in a weatherproof junction box near the pond, preferably in an inconspicuous spot (see illustration on facing page).

Even if you plan to simply plug the pump into an outlet, an electrician will have to install a weatherproof outdoor outlet box if the water feature is very far from the house. The outlet is usually mounted 10–12 inches off the ground on a metal post and can be tucked behind a shrub or plant.

■ **Wiring:** Protect buried wire by running it through PVC electrical conduit. Bury the conduit at least 18 inches deep.

Avoid using extension cords if the pool is distant from the electrical source. If you use one, it should be a heavy-duty, three-pronged, grounded, outdoor type of cord. Do not bury connecting ends because they are not waterproof. Instead, keep the connecting ends above ground and use a waterproof connector to avoid tripping the GFI circuit. Consider special ordering a pump with a longer cord to avoid the need for an extension cord.

Be sure your pond equipment won't overload the circuit. If you have any doubts, check with an electrician. Otherwise, you may have blown fuses and the expense and hassle of extra electrical work after you thought the installation was complete.

▲ **This softly-lit pond appears to be bathed in moonlight. Subtlety and restraint are key to effective lighting.**

Estimate the ability of the circuit to carry the additional load by adding up the total wattage of all bulbs and appliances that are plugged into the circuit, including those that are plugged in only occasionally. A 15-amp circuit can handle a continuous load of 1440 watts. A 20-amp circuit can handle 1920 watts.

> ## HINT
> Carefully read labels on electrical equipment to make sure they have been UL approved.

▼ **Electricity powers the bubbler fountain and the light, transforming a dark corner into an enchanting evening destination.**

LIGHTING

▲ Artfully positioned lights accent the water feature and the surrounding landscape, making the scene sparkle.

HINT

When positioning an in-water light to illuminate moving water, make sure the beam of light shines in the same direction as the water flows for the best effect.

used in the water should be made specifically for underwater use. For low-tech illumination, try solar-powered lights or floating votive platforms for candles.

Before you shop for water garden lights, experiment with different effects from a powerful flashlight or a spotlight on an extension cord (never place either in the water). Aim for restraint and subtlety. Don't let yourself get carried away with lighting that's more amusement park than understated elegance.

There are several types of in-water lights, and each creates its own special look, depending on how you position it (see the box on the opposite page). Most designs call for lights that have dark, subdued casings. Stainless steel or white casings can be obtrusive, especially during the daytime.

Fountain lights, either in white or colors, add drama to a spray. Some fountain lights also come equipped with transparent wheels of several colors. Colored light, however, should be used sparingly—it can easily become garish.

Many lights include built-in timers that allow you to automatically turn the lights on and off. You can also install an independent timer in the lighting setup. Timers not only save you the trouble of regulating the light, they also save on energy costs.

You can create amazing effects with water-feature lighting—make a fountain glow, illuminate an entire pond from within, highlight an attractive statue, or heighten the reflection of a particularly beautiful tree.

Water garden lights are available for installation as either in-water or outside-the-water lighting. All, however, should be connected to a GFI for safety, and those

INSTALLING LOW-VOLTAGE LIGHTING

Unlike regular 120-volt lights, installation of low-voltage landscape lights is a snap, even for beginners. And they're fairly safe because of their low voltage. Many low-voltage lighting systems are sold as kits, complete with instructions.

Hooking up a low-voltage system starts with installing a transformer, which reduces the regular household current from 120 volts to 12 volts. Install the transformer near the GFI receptacle closest to the water feature, following the manufacturer's instructions. Even 12-volt systems should use a GFI unit to prevent shocks. Most transformers are simply mounted next to an outlet and plugged into it.

Run exterior electrical cable from the transformer to the lights. It's important to choose a cable that has the right size of wire for the total wattage of the bulbs in the system (simply add the total watts of each bulb supplied by the cable): #14 wire can handle up to 144 watts, #12 wire up to 192 watts, and #10 wire up to 288 watts.

Bury the cable several inches under the ground, running it through a length of PVC pipe to provide extra protection from tillers and spades.

Then attach the lights to the cable. Some lights attach with clips; others must be wired into the system. Be sure to refer to the instructions.

WATER GARDEN LIGHTS

▲ FLOATING

Drifting on top of the water, floating lights create a festive atmosphere. Some floating light fixtures are ornamental; in the shape of lily pads, for example. To hold the lights in one place, anchor the cord with smooth-edged brick or stone.

▲ SUBMERGED

Made for underwater use, submerged lights illuminate the pool or draw attention to features outside the pool, such as special plants or statues. They also add drama when installed under fountains or waterfalls. Underwater lighting is available for both floodlighting and spotlighting effects, which are both diffused.

▲ FLOODLIGHT

Use the wide beam of a floodlight to illuminate large areas. Inside a pond or pool, it can make the body of water seem to glow from within. Outside the pool, it's best to restrict lighting to a seating area, such as a deck, because it produces a glare if directed at a sharp angle to the water. If used outside the pool, position it to shoot across the water at a low angle.

▲ SPOTLIGHT

The tight beam of a spotlight can shine upward to highlight a specific feature. Place it beneath an attractive element, such as a waterfall, and the element will appear to glow. When carefully positioned under the water, a spotlight can create a reflection of the feature it illuminates. Outside the water, aim it to highlight a feature in the water or place it under statues, trees, or other large poolside plants.

▲ POND JET

Pond jet lights, also called fountain spray lights, dramatically accentuate the fountain and add magic to the nighttime water garden. These floating lights are sold in sets of three, or in a kit with a submersible pump and a timer, which work in tandem with the lights.

▲ OUT-OF-POOL LIGHTS

Low-voltage lights installed along a path or at the water's edge are called out-of-pool lights. This category includes spotlights, floodlights, and other light fixtures located outside the water.

Placing lights

The one rule in placing lights is to never let them shine directly on the water, because they will create a harsh glare. In-pond lights need fairly clear water to be effective. Murky water blocks too much light and considerably diminishes the light's effectiveness. If you have fish in your water garden, leave dark areas where they can retreat from the light. Fish need plenty of crevices for refuge. And never light up the entire pond, especially for the whole night.

Whenever possible, position out-of-water lights to conceal their housings and cords: underneath a deck, behind a rock, or tucked into the foliage of a shrub. Whatever type of lighting you choose, be sensitive to its effect on the neighbors. Don't let the lights shine in their windows.

DIGGING

The most daunting part of creating a large garden pond is the digging. But with some advance planning—and when done properly—digging can be downright fun.

Advance planning

When planning your garden pond, take into consideration how much digging you can do and adjust either the size of the water garden or the amount of work you do alone. Digging even a small pool is not a job for a person with a history of back pain or heart problems.

■ **Getting help:** If you can't dig it yourself, consider hiring a neighborhood teen, or get friends and relatives to help. For very large projects, you may want to hire a backhoe operator. As a rule, water gardens with a surface area of less than 250 square feet are most economically dug by hand; larger projects are best done with a backhoe.

■ **Time:** Allow plenty of time for digging, considering both pool size and soil type. A small, 18-inch-deep, 3×5-foot pool in

DIGGING A POOL

1 Mark the outline of the pond with a garden hose or rope, or sprinkle a line of flour, fine soil, or garden lime. Live with the outline for a week or so to discover how the new feature fits into the landscape and how it will affect traffic patterns.

2 Remove turf. Use it to fill bare spots in the lawn or set it aside in a pile of its own to compost. If you have a large quantity, use it as the base of a berm or a raised bed. Stack the turf in the spot for the berm, then cover with several inches of topsoil.

3 As you dig, keep the pond edge level. If it is not level, the liner will show. Rest a carpenter's level on a straight board laid across the pond to check it. Work all around the pond, carefully checking every side of the pool so that there are no surprises.

4 Create a spot to overwinter plants and fish. In cold areas, you'll need a zone in the pool that won't freeze. It should be up to 3 feet deep and as wide as it is deep. Be sure this deep zone isn't in the same spot you want to place a pump or fountain.

5 Dig the shelf for the marginal plants about 8 to 12 inches deep. Position the marginal-plant shelf so that the plants frame your view of the water garden. Then dig a ledge for the edging as deep as the edging material and slightly less wide.

6 Toss the excavated soil into a wheelbarrow to protect your lawn. If it's in good condition, use the soil to fill in other low spots in the landscape, to build up a slope for a waterfall, or haul it away to a construction site that needs fill dirt.

PROPER DIGGING TECHNIQUE

Digging your garden pond correctly will save you a lot of minor aches and pains as well as possible serious injury.

■ **Wear the proper clothes:** A good pair of heavy boots helps you plant your feet, keeps you from slipping, and lets you work more efficiently, reducing fatigue. While digging, be sure to keep a straight back and good posture. Don't stoop or let your shoulders slump. Also, keep your knees bent at all times. This distributes weight to your legs. Lift with your legs, not just with your back.

■ **Work the soil when it's moist:** To minimize the effort of cutting into the earth without adding much weight to the soil, avoid working excessively wet soil. Scoop up small amounts of soil at a time. Keep loads on the spade reasonably small to prevent strain. Grip the spade close to the blade to give yourself better control.

■ **Bend your knees:** Don't stretch out your body to toss the soil in a pile far away; this will overextend your back. As soon as the hole is large enough, step into it and work from the inside.

▲ **Wrong way to dig: Poor posture and improper attire lead to problems.**

▲ **Right way to dig: Keep your back straight and knees bent. Wear protective clothes.**

sandy soil may take only an hour or so, while a 24-inch-deep, 6×10-foot pool in clay can take a day or more. Pace yourself. Even if you're in good shape, divide larger projects into one-hour increments with a half-hour rest in between so you don't strain your back.

■ **Tools:** Make sure your tools are in excellent condition and well-suited to the task. Start with a sharp pointed-blade spade. You'll also need a wheelbarrow for hauling dirt and possibly a truck to haul away soil.

It's best to dig when the soil is moist but not wet. That allows the spade to cut through the soil neatly, and the soil isn't overly heavy. If the weather has been dry, you can moisten the top foot or so of soil by soaking it with water from a hose. Let the soil drain before you start digging.

Digging in

Start by marking the site with a garden hose, rope, or garden lime. Then fine-tune the outline with stakes (every foot or so) and twine. Cut along the outline with a spade, and then remove the top layer of sod. However, if you're going to use turf as edging, cut the sod approximately 4 inches in from the outline of the pond. Remove the sod inside the outline and peel back the 4-inch strip. After installing the liner, flip the sod strip back over it.

To edge with stones or other material, dig an outwardly sloping shelf 6–8 inches wide by 2 inches deep for the liner and the

edging. The trench should be deep enough for the edging stones to sit flush with the ground or 3–4 inches deep for a concrete footing for edges that will get heavy traffic.

With the sod removed, mark the outlines for marginal shelves, and then begin digging from the center outward. Dig 2 inches deeper than the pool depth to allow for sand underlayment (less for other materials). As you dig, angle the sides slightly, about 20 degrees, and make sure the edges of the pond are level or the liner will show. With a small project, place a carpenter's level on a straight piece of 2×4, checking all around the pond.

For a large project, put a stake in the center of the pond with its top at the planned water level. Rest one end of a long straight board on the stake and the other end on the edge of the pool. Check the level. Rotate the board a few feet, again noting the level. Repeat until you return to the starting point.

Use the removed sod to patch bare spots in the yard or add the sod to a compost pile. If the topsoil is in reasonably good condition, add it to the vegetable garden, spread it on flowerbeds, or create new beds and berms. If you're installing a rigid liner, set aside the soil to backfill around the liner. Put the soil in a wheelbarrow or on a large tarp or piece of plastic to protect the lawn. Discard clay-laden subsoil or use it to build up a slope for a waterfall. Dump larger amounts at a landfill.

HINT

Keep good-quality topsoil and poorer quality subsoil separate by tossing them onto two different pieces of plastic or tarp. Reuse the good soil in your landscape. Discard the poor-quality subsoil.

WORKING SAFELY WITH ROCKS

Working in the garden is a wonderful opportunity to enjoy the physical benefits normally associated with a workout in the gym, but there is also the possibility of injuring yourself. Fortunately, by following a few simple guidelines, you can minimize the risks of sprains and strains when you're digging and pulling, bending and stretching, moving rocks, or lifting heavy pots. As writer Barbara Damrosch put it, "People who view gardening as backbreaking are probably using their backs when they should use their heads." If you are building your own pond, you will be doing a lot of digging and lifting, including moving and positioning heavy rocks.

Dress appropriately

■ **Shoes:** Sandals may be fine when you're tying up the tomatoes or pulling the odd weed, but sturdy, fully enclosed shoes or boots are safer when you're digging and moving rocks. If you have a pair of leather boots, or better yet steel-toed boots, wear them. You want that extra protection if you accidentally drop a rock on your foot or miss your aim with the pick.

■ **Gloves:** Heavy-duty leather work gloves are important to protect your hands from scratches and abrasion, and also as a little extra padding in case your hand gets trapped under a stone.

▲ **Use a dolly to haul large rocks long distances across the yard to the pond.**

◄ **Lift with your back straight and knees slightly bent to avoid injury to your back.**

■ **Eye protection:** It's a good idea to wear safety goggles, especially if you are using a pickax or mattock to loosen soil and rocks and when loading and unloading rock loads. In either case, chunks of soil or rock chips may fly into your eye, causing serious injury if you are unprotected.

■ **Sunscreen:** Even on an overcast day, ultraviolet light rays can cause sunburn. Wear sunscreen on your exposed skin, and a hat with a brim for extra protection on your face.

■ **Knee pads:** If your work involves a lot of kneeling, invest in a pair of knee pads. To reduce strain, kneel on one knee, then the other, then crouch for a bit, then squat.

■ **Dust mask:** If you are working with material made up of fine particles, such as cement, peat moss, and some fertilizers, wear a dust mask.

■ **Back belt:** Finally, if you know you are prone to back injury or strain, wear a back belt to remind you of the proper back position for lifting and to help support your abdominal muscles. Don't forget to tighten it when you're doing the heavy lifting, and to loosen it when you're resting or working on something else.

Lifting techniques

■ **Use your legs:** Your leg muscles are bigger and stronger than your back muscles, so make them do the work when you lift. Face your hips and feet toward the object you are lifting or moving. Keep your weight over your hips, which are your center of gravity, and bend at the knees, rather than the waist. Lift in a slow, even motion, and

with well-made, well-balanced garden tools. A heavy, long-handled shovel may be perfect for a tall, strong person, but completely wrong for a shorter person with less body strength. Use tools scaled to your body size, and weighted to be comfortable to lift. Useful digging tools include a shovel, spading fork, pickax or mattock, and a pry or digging bar to lever rocks into position.

Vary activities

Holding the same position for an extended period causes cramping, and repeating the same motion causes strains and stress on ligaments and joints. Yet gardeners often get so absorbed in a gardening task, or so driven to complete it in a specified period of time, that they forget the importance of taking time to stretch, of changing their working position, and of varying the task.

Instead of digging and hauling stones for six straight hours, then waking up the next day so stiff and sore you cannot face working in the garden again for several weeks, alternate between strenuous tasks and easier ones, and between jobs that require different muscle groups so you don't overtax yourself. Remember, even with all of this strenuous activity, gardening is still a leisure pursuit. Take stretching breaks to relieve cramped muscles, and drink plenty of water.

▲ Once the rock is close to its final position, use a pry bar to maneuver it into place.

don't twist your body. If you must turn, do so with your feet, not from your waist. Keep the heavy object close to your body at waist level to reduce the leverage on your spine. Also make sure your fingers are positioned so you won't pinch them when you set the load down. While lifting, inhale and exhale deeply to get oxygen to those working muscles.

■ **Push, don't pull:** If you have a choice between pulling and pushing a heavy object, push. It's natural to use your legs when you push something, but you'll tend to put your back into the task of pulling.

Know your limits. Don't overdo it. Size up a load, and if necessary get someone to help you if it's too heavy.

If you need to move a heavy object across the garden, inspect the route where the load will be carried. Be sure to especially look for tripping hazards and make sure you have adequate room along the route to maneuver safely.

Tools for digging, lifting, and shifting

Humans set themselves apart from most animals by the ability to use tools. If you need to shift large amounts of earth or rock, use a wheelbarrow. Move large rocks or plants with large root balls on a dolly or wheeled platform, or drag them along the ground on a strong tarpaulin.

■ **Choose properly sized tools:** Digging is much more pleasant—and easier to do—

▶ A heavy tarp makes it easy to slide a rock across level ground to the work site.

Constructing a Pool With a Flexible Liner

First, outline the pool's shape on the planned site. Use a garden hose or rope to outline a naturalistic, informal shape. Confirm the planned length and width using a measuring tape. Observe the layout over the next few days; modify it if you wish. When you're satisfied, use powdered limestone or flour to mark the final shape.

■ **Laying out formal pools:** Marking the perimeter of a formal pool requires stakes and string to create straight lines, carefully measured angles, and perfect circles. Make rectangles or squares using triangulation (see the illustration below). Use a stake to mark the center of a circular pool. Attach the stake to a length of string equal to the radius of the circle. Walk around the stake with the string outstretched fully, marking the circular perimeter with flour or powdered limestone.

▲ To create a circular layout of a pool, place one stake in the center. Scribe a circle with another stake and rope. Mark the outline with flour.

Excavating the site

A friend or hired help makes this laborious task easier. A professional pond installer comes equipped to deal with unforeseen obstructions that may lurk under the soil's surface. Or, if you are able to operate it efficiently, rent a backhoe if it's warranted by the size of the pond and its accessibility.

Before you start digging, check with local utilities to ensure that there are no buried cables. Be prepared with a variety of shovels, a pick, a digging bar, garden rakes, a soil tamp, and a wheelbarrow. If you plan to excavate an area of existing lawn, strip off the sod before you dig and remove any soil. Roll up the sod and save it in a shady place for use around the edge of the installed pond or elsewhere. Plan where you will move the excavated material. Some or all of the soil might be used to build a waterfall.

■ **Determine the lowest perimeter point:** Unless part or all of the pool will be located aboveground, this point defines the level for the top edge of the pond. Measure the pond depth from this point. Begin digging at the center and work out to the edges, being careful not to dig beyond the perimeter. Form the sidewalls carefully.

▲ To create a right angle, mark out a triangle with sides of 3, 4, and 5 feet.

Excavate 8–10 inches deep where you plan to create a narrow shelf to support a stone veneer for hiding the pond liner; make the shelf 6–12 inches wide (depending on the size of the stones used as veneer). Coping or edging will eventually rest on top of the stone veneer. The wider you make the shelf, the greater the loss of pool space. If you plan to use cement blocks to make the sidewalls for the pool, excavate for the blocks. The depth of the excavation depends on how deep the blocks will be set in the ground. Excavate 2 inches wider than the width of the blocks to allow room to work.

Leveling the pool

Ensure that the pond's top edge is level by laying a 2×4 across the excavation with the ends of the board on opposite sides of the pond. Set a carpenter's level on top of the board to confirm that the perimeter is level. For pools too large to use this method, use a central stake as a leveling reference. Extend a string to each point being checked, verifying the level each time with a carpenter's level. Survey equipment (available for rent in metropolitan areas) accurately confirms level using a theodolite or laser transit. Check and recheck the depth and level as you continue to excavate. Allow yourself a margin of error plus or minus ¼ inch of level.

■ **Build the sidewalls:** Form sidewalls with a slight pitch outward from bottom to top—a 10–15-degree slope works well for firm soil. Sandy soil works better with a 20–30-degree slope. Visually check the soil to determine whether it keeps the form you've excavated. If it lacks stability and slides down, make the slope less steep.

If the soil is not firm, tamp the edges. If you want steeper walls than the soil permits, consider forming the sides with cement blocks. Remove all rocks and tree roots from the sides and base. Fill any depressions with sand or soil.

If you live where summers are mild (few days above 80°F) or where winters are mild (few days with ice on the pool), you may want to include planting shelves. Excavate these as you shape the sidewalls. Planting shelves typically measure 10–16 inches wide and sit about 10–12 inches below the water's surface.

Make a small depression in the deepest area for future draining with a pump. The bottom should slope slightly, at the rate of 1 inch per 10 feet, toward the depression.

▶ As you excavate your pool, create sloping sides with a flat top for edging. Dig a shelf for potted plants and a deep spot at the lowest point of the pond for drainage.

◀ Successful pool construction requires that the top is level. For a small area such as this, put a stake in the hole and lay a carpenter's level across. Continue to check for level as you go.

▶ Start with a 2-inch layer of sand on the pool bottom. Next, put down an underlayment such as newspaper, old carpet, or geotextile.

▽ A water garden, unlike most other landscape projects, looks complete during its first growing season.

INSTALLING FLEXIBLE LINER

Flexible liner has become popular largely because it's easy to install. However, you must install it properly to prevent the liner from showing. Liners exposed to ultraviolet (UV) light can deteriorate quickly and develop leaks.

Preparation

■ **Liner:** After digging and ensuring that the edges of the pond are level, remove anything with rough edges that might puncture the liner—roots, rocks, debris, or buried shards of glass.

Spread the liner out in the sun for an hour or two to let it soften, which makes it much easier to work with. If you need to seam two pieces, do it now, using solvent cement or adhesive designed especially for this purpose.

Avoid dragging the liner over the ground or rocks and gravel, which may cause rips or punctures.

■ **Underlayment:** Underlayment cushions the liner, which extends its life, and prevents rocks and twigs from puncturing it. Use a layer of damp sand on horizontal surfaces, or old carpet, or underlayment made specifically for use with flexible liner. The layer should be ½–2 inches thick, depending on the material.

Cover the sides as well as the bottom of the pool with the underlayment. Many lining materials are easier to work with if you wet them first, especially when applying them up the sides of the pool. Also, cut triangles in fabric materials to fit the contours.

Installation

■ **Spreading:** Depending on the size of your garden pond, spreading the liner may take one or several people. Try flapping it like a sheet (up and down) to force air under the liner and help it float into place. Smooth out the liner and fold it neatly to fit into the contours and corners of the pond as much as possible. Don't stretch the liner.

Leave a little wrinkle of extra liner in the bottom of the pond—"pinch an inch" here

▲ **Installing flexible liner is fairly simple. Although one person can accomplish the job, it goes faster with two.**

or there. This allows the liner to spread a little when the soil settles, which is particularly wise in earthquake-prone areas. Leave as much excess liner as possible (at least 6 inches) over the outside edge of the pool. Use bricks or stones to temporarily hold it in place.

■ **Adding water:** Fill the pool with a few inches of water, and then readjust the liner, once again pleating, folding, or arranging it to get as smooth a fit as possible. Move the bricks if needed. Fill the pond about halfway and adjust the liner and bricks again. Folds and wrinkles will always occur. Once adjustments are made, fill the pond almost completely.

■ **Edging:** Cover the edges of the liner with soil (or concrete if the edge around the pond must support heavy traffic or a heavy edging material). Then you can install the edging, letting it overhang the pond by at least 2–3 inches. Trim the liner with heavy scissors or a utility knife, leaving enough excess to protect the edging shelf.

HINT

When it's time to install edging, keep flexible liner in place while you work by pushing large nails through the edge of the liner into the soil every foot or so.

Other uses for liner

To repair a cracked concrete pond, drain it, remove any gravel, sand, or other grit, and place an underlayment over the concrete surface. Cushioning the liner with an underlayment is especially important because concrete can abrade holes in the liner. Position the liner, trim it to size, and then lay new edging. To line a wooden whiskey barrel or box with flexible liner, use the same procedure, but staple the liner in place above the water line.

EDGING TIP

Here's a good way to prevent the liner from showing. Dig the edging shelf deep enough for a double layer of flagstones, cut stones, bricks, or other edging. Lay the first layer of edging, and then wrap the liner behind and over the first layer as shown and top with the second. Water can now be filled to the middle of the first layer of edging. With one layer of edging, the water can be filled only a little below the bottom of the edging.

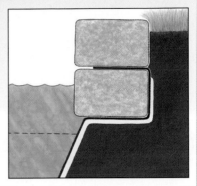

INSTALLING LINER

1 Excavate the hole for the water garden. Cushion the hole with underlayment. This can be moist sand, old carpet, or underlayment specifically made for water gardens. Cover both the bottom and the sides. Cut triangles at corners and curves of the underlayment to help fit contours.

2 Position liner. Let the liner warm in the sun for at least an hour to soften. Drape it loosely in the hole, arranging and pleating as needed. (This may be a job for two or more people.) Anchor the sides with bricks or stones, taking care to not stretch the liner.

3 Adjust the liner. Add a few inches of water to the pool to settle the liner. Pleat and tuck the liner, as necessary, to make it fit the contours and corners of the water feature.

4 Install edging. Fill the pond with a few more inches of water. Adjust liner, then fill the pool to just below the edging shelf. Trim the liner.

5 Complete the surrounding landscape. Do a final trim of the liner. You can pat a little soil in behind the edging to conceal any visible liner.

BOG GARDENS

◀ Bog plants are functional as well as attractive. They act as natural filters to keep the water clean and also provide food and shelter for wildlife.

COMMON BOG PLANTS

Aquatic grasses
Cardinal flower
Cattail
Creeping Jenny
Horsetail
Marsh marigold
Pickerel weed
Arrowhead
Umbrella palm
Water iris
Water canna

A bog garden is a wonderful solution to several landscaping challenges. A freestanding bog garden creates the perfect microclimate for moisture-loving plants. A bog garden attached to a pool or pond makes the pond look more natural, providing a transition to the rest of the landscape and attracting wildlife. A bog garden is also a solution for a low or chronically wet spot where plants that prefer drier soil do not thrive.

Bog gardens are among the easiest water features to install and maintain. Simply put, they are beds of moisture-retentive soil spread over a pond liner, which helps the soil hold water.

Most plants that do well as marginals in a pond also do well as bog plants. Gardeners in moist climates can create bog gardens for plants with high moisture requirements—such as water iris, cattail, umbrella palm, and aquatic grasses. Gardeners in dry climates, especially those in the West, can use a bog garden to grow plants with more modest water requirements that would otherwise not do well in their region.

ANATOMY OF A BOG GARDEN

MOISTURE-LOVING PLANTS
Most like full sun

SOIL OR STONE
Covers edge; hides flexible liner

WATER
3" layer for mosquito fish

SOIL
Mimics that of bogs found in nature

FLEXIBLE LINER

SAND

PEA GRAVEL

Usable locations

If you have a low spot that naturally collects water, it may be the perfect site for a bog garden. Areas where the soil is heavy clay with slow drainage, or low-lying areas that collect rain are good possibilities. Even a location near a downspout or other clean water drainage could serve as a bog garden. Also consider creating a mini bog garden in a container; simply plug any holes and plant accordingly. Because most plants for bog gardens are sun lovers, locate the garden on a site that receives six or more hours of direct light a day.

Freestanding or connected?

You can create the bog so its water supply is completely independent of the pond, or erect a small, water-permeable dam to allow water to percolate into the bog. A bog that is independent of a pond has an advantage over a connected bog—it's easier to maintain the ideal moisture level in the bog. Just water when the soil seems too dry. Also, you can fertilize an independent bog with less danger that chemicals will seep into the pond.

To create an independent bog, build an earthen dam between it and the pond, making sure the dam comes up to or above the water level. Cover the dam with flexible liner, disguise it with stone, and water the bog independently.

▶ Bog gardens make a good transition between the water and the rest of the landscape. Yellow flag irises, shown in the foreground, are one of the most popular plants for bog gardens.

HINT

If you're concerned about soil eroding into a pond, cover the surface of the soil surrounding the bog with an inch or so of sand or gravel.

◀ A bog garden's marshlike conditions allow you to grow a wonderful array of plants that otherwise would not thrive in a home garden.

To interconnect the pond with the bog, continue the flexible liner from the pool into the bog (at a depth of 6–18 inches). Construct a stone dam between the bog and the pond, on top of the liner. Leave a hole or two in the dam so water can seep in, or insert a couple of lengths of PVC pipe through the dam. You can line the inside face of the rock dam with plastic liner so soil from the bog doesn't wash into the pond, leaving the holes or pipe uncovered.

Specific needs for bogs

■ **Liner and drainage:** The bottom layer of a bog should consist of an inch or two of pea gravel, which allows water to drain away from the soil when the soil is saturated. Cover the pea gravel with geotextile to prevent soil from washing down into it.

Because the liner isn't exposed to sun—its edges are buried just under the soil surface—you can use inexpensive polyethylene sheeting, but regular pond liner will last longer.

Bog plants need moisture; they thrive in up to 3 inches of standing water. Avoid holes in the liner which may create too much drainage. Drying out will more likely kill bog plants than will excess moisture.

Exercise care when increasing the drainage of a bog that is fed by a pool or stream. If the bog drains too much, the rest of the water feature will also lose water.

In dry climates, consider an irrigation system for your bog. The simplest system is a length of soaker hose or perforated pipe along the bottom of the bog. Run the soaker hose or pipe to the soil surface and connect it to a garden hose to allow water to seep slowly and evenly into the soil.

■ **Soil:** Soil in natural bogs is high in humus. But the high level of decaying organic matter attracts insects, creates unpleasant odors, and may rot plants. Use high quality topsoil for your bog garden, and avoid adding additional organic matter.

Sphagnum peat moss from natural bogs is sometimes used in bogs, since it absorbs and holds many times its weight in water. It might, however, inhibit the growth of some plants, so use it sparingly until you get to know the plants.

▲ **Water iris, sedge *(Carex)*, and rodgersia are easy bog plants. Although the flowers will fade, the swordlike iris foliage adds interest throughout the season.**

HINT

If you install an irrigation system in your bog, attach a quick-release hose coupler to the end of the system and the end of your hose for ease of use.

■ **Plants:** Many plants that thrive in shallow water also do well in bogs. Marginals, such as yellow flag and cardinal flower, do especially well in bogs. However, be ready to experiment to see what plants do best in your particular bog. (See pages 98–108 for a description of many marginals and bog plants.) Soil, moisture, and regional climate can vary radically from bog garden to bog garden. If one plant doesn't work, try another. If the soil mix is too rich and rots the roots, work in a high-quality topsoil to lighten it.

It's important to keep your bog constantly moist, which can be a challenge during late summer. Because some of the plants will grow in standing water but others won't, test for soil dryness to a depth of at least 4 or 5 inches. If the soil is not almost soggy, water deeply.

Fertilize your bog garden periodically with slow-release fertilizers. Avoid using compost. Excess organic matter can attract bugs and create odor problems.

1 Dig a hole 6–18 inches deep in an area receiving at least six hours of sun a day. A low-lying or poorly drained area is perfect. So is a site next to a pool or pond, where it's easy to keep the bog's soil moist.

2 Line the bog. Spread inexpensive liner over the hole. In heavy clay soil, pierce it with a garden fork every 3 feet or so. In sandy soils, do not pierce the liner. Spread 1–2 inches of pea gravel on the bottom of the hole. Trim the liner so it will be concealed under edging materials.

3 After digging the adjoining pond, create a dam between the pond and the bog. Either build one of earth while you're digging or make one of rocks positioned between the bog and pond. Place liner against the rocks to prevent soil from washing into the pond.

4 Fill the bog with high-quality, moisture-retentive topsoil. Plant moisture-loving species in the bog and water them well. Fertilize occasionally with slow-release fertilizer.

INSTALLING A PREFORMED LINER

HOW TO INSTALL A PREFORMED LINER

1 Position the liner where you plan to locate the pond, using bricks if necessary to keep it level. Then pound stakes in place around the liner and use them as a guide to mark the exact outline. If the pool is small, make a template by tracing around the lip instead.

2 Dig out the shape of the liner, making it 2 inches wider and 2–3 inches deeper than the actual liner. Conform your digging to the shape of shelves and deep zones, measuring depth, width, and level frequently. Monitor your work by lowering the liner into place and making adjustments.

3 Remove any sharp objects or stones left on the bottom of the hole once it is dug. Then cover the bottom with moist sand, fine soil, or a combination of the two. Smooth the sand with a rake or short board to level the bottom. Tamp it down firmly and check the level once again.

4 Lower the liner into place, checking the level with a carpenter's level set on the rim of the pool. You may need to remove the liner several times to make depth adjustments or to make the entire perimeter level.

5 Begin backfilling. Tamp the soil with a shovel handle or 2×4 as you work. Backfill again and add 4 inches of water, keeping the water level no higher than the backfill. Repeat until the pool is filled.

Excavate the pond

Although a rigid liner is a little more difficult to install than a flexible one, it's still relatively simple. The key is ensuring the liner is level through the entire process.

■ **Mark the outline:** Start by putting the liner in position before you begin to dig. You may need to use bricks to hold up portions of the liner if it has varying depths. Level the liner as much as possible. Trace around the perimeter of the liner. Then pound stakes every foot or so around the liner following the contour of its lip. Further mark around it with rope, a garden hose, flour, or lime.

■ **Dig the hole:** Dig the hole to conform to the shape of the liner, measuring frequently to check depths and widths. The hole needs to be larger than the liner—allow an extra 2 inches around its perimeter and 2–3 inches at the bottom. Remove any rocks or sharp objects as you work. Set the liner in place to see if it fits, and make adjustments as needed.

■ **Keep it level:** Remove the liner and fill the bottom of the hole with a combination of sand and fine soil. Level this mix with a short board (called a screed), and then firmly tamp the soil to create a stable base. Make sure the bottom, marginal shelves, and edges are still absolutely level in all directions after tamping. For large ponds, set the carpenter's level on a straight piece of lumber to check for level.

■ **Position the liner:** Place the liner in the hole, pressing it down gently so that it fits snugly in the deepest areas. Recheck for level. You may need to remove the liner several times to make adjustments.

■ **Backfill around the liner:** Once the pond is perfectly level, fill it with 4 inches of water to stabilize it. Then begin backfilling around the sides of the pond with a mixture of sand and fine soil, checking for levelness as you go. Tamp the soil-sand mixture in gently with a shovel handle or the end of a 2×4. Be certain to fill all voids and pockets, especially around and under the marginal shelves of varying depths.

Fill the pond with another 4 inches of water. Never allow the water level to be higher than the backfill because the liner may bulge outward. Add more backfill and more water. Repeat until you have completed the backfilling and the pond is full to within a couple of inches of the top.

Edging

Make preparations for the edging. If the liner has a flat lip, work a foundation of crushed stone topped with damp sand under the lip and around liner edges. Then position the stone or other edging on top of the edge.

If the lip is concave or otherwise can't hold the weight of the edging (or heavy traffic), dig and pour a 3–4-inch deep concrete footing that extends beyond and over the top of the lip. Embed the edging in the concrete, overhanging the inside of the liner by 1–2 inches. The weight of the edging will be supported by the foundation of mortar.

After the mortar has cured (24-48 hours), scrub with muriatic acid or household vinegar to neutralize the lime. Drain the pond (runoff from the acid will make the water toxic), rinse, and refill.

PREFORMED LINERS ABOVEGROUND

Working with a rigid liner is even easier and faster when building an aboveground pool.

It's ideal—but not absolutely necessary—to partially bury the liner so that its marginal shelves are flush with the soil surface. (Partially burying it helps stabilize water temperatures.) Dig the hole 2 inches wider on the sides and 2 inches deeper on the bottom. Add sand, tamp it down, then position the liner, making sure it's exactly level. Fill the unit with 4 inches of water to stabilize it. Backfill to ground level, tamping with a 2×4 or the back of your spade.

Then add the siding, which can be a wood frame, stacked flagstones, cut stone, concrete pavers, wooden flower-border edging, logs set on end, or other materials. As you install the siding, backfill along the sides of the rigid liner with soil and moist sand to support the sides of the liner. Depending on the type of siding, you may want to leave pockets of soil between the liner and the siding in which to insert plants to soften the liner edges.

If the pond is built into the side of a hill, be sure to set it out 6–12 inches from the slope to prevent erosion. To prevent the pond from sliding out of place, it's an especially good idea to partially bury the bottom of the liner that's placed on a hill. Backfill around the bottom of the pond and the side of the pond that faces the hill.

▲ Disguise the sides of an aboveground rigid liner by covering them with a wood frame, stacked flagstones, or concrete retaining wall blocks.

INSTALLING ABOVEGROUND POOLS

▲ **When skillfully designed and surrounded by stacked stone, an aboveground pool blends beautifully into the landscape.**

Even if you don't have hard-to-dig, problem soil, an aboveground pool may suit you. Not only are aboveground ponds good options where digging would be difficult, but they are also appealing in their ability to raise the water up close, which is especially nice near a patio or other sitting area.

Raised and semi-raised water features tend to take longer than sunken ponds to build and usually cost more. However, they're less likely to become cluttered with blowing debris or eroding soil.

■ **Types of pools:** Aboveground pools are as varied as the gardeners who install them. The only requirement is that they be built from materials sturdy enough to withstand the outward pressure of water.

Aboveground water features are often made of brick, an excellent material in formal gardens or in landscapes that already contain a lot of brick. Concrete block—veneered with stucco, brick, tile, or stone—is another option. Wood timbers stacked upon each other, lumber fashioned into a charming box, or logs stacked on end in a row provide other possibilities for aboveground pools. Raised water features can also be made of cut or natural stone.

■ **Height:** The height of an aboveground pool can vary from just 1 foot to much higher. For a pool that's completely aboveground, the ideal height is between 24 and 30 inches, especially if you want passersby to see the fish or to be able to sit on the edge. The pool should be a minimum of 18 inches deep. For a pool that rises above ground less than that height, partially excavate the pool to make

MAKING A STONE-SIDED POOL

1 Rigid liner works well for creating aboveground ponds with stone sides. Flexible liner can tear in such installations. Choose a fiberglass pool with a flat lip, which will best withstand weather extremes and support the weight of stone edging. For the easiest, least expensive, and lowest-maintenance pond, dig a hole and sink the liner to the depth of its marginal shelves. By burying part of the liner, you minimize masonry work and stabilize pool temperatures in summer.

2 Experiment before you start—lay a trial side of stone until the height and inset are correct. Set each course of stone in slightly toward the liner. Backfill behind each course as you go. Lay the first course far enough away from the liner to allow for sufficient inset.

3 Carefully backfill under the lip of the liner with a mixture of moist sand and fine soil. For additional strength, pack concrete under the lip. Conceal the liner edge by slightly overhanging the edging to the inside of the pond. Position the edging so as little weight as possible rests on the liner lip.

MAKING A WOOD-SIDED POOL

1 Build wood-sided pools with rot-resistant wood and rust-resistant hardware. Measure and cut all materials before assembly. The pool shown here will be built with flexible liner. If using a rigid liner, allow room for backfill. Predrill at the corners and at 8–10-inch intervals along the wall for corner and side ties. Use all-thread, which is long steel rod threaded along its length, or concrete rebar for the ties. Bury the first course in the soil slightly, by half its height, to improve stability.

2 If the pool is large or will sit completely above ground, add a 2-inch layer of sand on the bottom. (Use plywood for the bottom of small pools on a deck or patio.) Insulate and protect the pool by covering interior sides of the box with old carpet, water garden underlayment, or smooth plywood. As you construct the pool, check frequently to make certain all sides are level.

3 Position the liner, pleating carefully. Fill the bottom 4 inches, do a final check of level, and reposition the liner if necessary. (Even a very small pool weighs hundreds of pounds when filled, so do any repositioning now.) Then fill the pool halfway. Staple the liner in place above the final water level, being careful that no stretching of the liner will take place once it's filled. Create a cap along the top to give the pool a finished look and conceal the liner edge.

it 18 inches deep. By doing this, the feature will be better insulated from the elements.

Footings: A masonry aboveground pool will need a concrete footing around the perimeter of its base. The depth of the footing depends on your climate, but it may need to be as deep as 2 feet in colder regions. Check local codes for proper depth. You can pour the footing directly into a trench; in soft soil you may need to build wooden forms with 2×4s for the footing. Either way, make sure the footing is perfectly level from one side to the other.

Materials: Wooden raised pools are simple to make; masonry projects require more time and skill. Structures made of wood are most successful when constructed from pressure-treated lumber or redwood to prevent rot. The wood should be relatively smooth to prevent flexible liner from ripping during installation.

No matter what material you use for the sides of your raised feature, the pool will need to be underlaid and lined. Rigid liner works well for raised gardens, but flexible liner offers more options for style and shape, and is limited only by your imagination. Staple the liner to the edges of wooden structures or glue it to them with silicone sealant. In masonry projects, sandwich the liner between the last course of brick and the cap.

▲ The wood siding anchors this pool into the landscape, matching the steps and planter boxes.

EDGING

Selecting and installing the right edging for your water garden is critical. Edging not only hides the liner, it also defines the style of your garden pond and sets its mood.

Rough boulders, especially native stone, look just right around a naturalistic pond or stream. Turf is good for a formal pool set in the middle of a lawn. Brick and cut stone—rectangular or square—lend themselves to formal garden ponds. Flagstone works well in informal water gardens.

Select edging with a character compatible with the materials or landscape that surround the pool. Flagstone works best when there is similar stone in the landscape. Brick is attractive in a garden pool set near a brick house or patio.

You might edge the pond with hardscape, cutting it into or locating it adjacent to a deck or patio, for example. Such installations are easiest to create when designed from the ground up with the deck or patio, but most existing structures can be retrofitted with a water feature of some kind. Before you choose edging, consider its use, cost, and installation.

Turf

Turf makes a striking edging for formal pools set in a flat stretch of lawn. It is a good choice to use around inground preformed liners that can't support much weight. The site for a turf-edged pond should be flat (or made so by filling in with soil) because on slopes, water in the pond levels out, exposing the liner.

Use turf as edging only when you can keep the surrounding lawn in excellent

▲ **Concrete pavers suit this pocket-sized water garden. They add a sense of age, as if the water feature has always been part of the landscape.**

HINT

After installing the liner, make sure the water in the pond will cover it entirely. Check the edges (before laying the edging material) to make sure they're level by setting a carpenter's level on a 2×4 laid across the pond.

◄ **Turf is a great choice to edge an inground pool when the ground is flat and the surrounding lawn will not have to bear excessive foot traffic.**

health. But take great care when applying fertilizer and pesticides around the water feature with a spreader. Although these materials don't usually run off turf, the spreader can fling them into the water. Nitrogen and phosphorus in the fertilizer can promote growth of algae in the pond. And fish are highly sensitive to many pesticides, including some organic ones.

It costs little to install a turf edging. And installation is easy; simply pat soil over the liner edge and toss some seed on it. Installing sod requires a little more effort but is worth it—sod keeps soil from eroding into the pond.

A turf edging does, however, take extra care. The shallow rooting area means roots burn easily, so don't let the grass dry out. Keep clippings out of the water when you mow. Hand trim around the pond every week or so.

Flagstone

Flagstone works well with boulders, gravel, sand, or rock in naturalistic settings. It is easy to install as an edging and ideal for a variety of water features—including those on slopes—because you can stack it. Flagstone is excellent for securing flexible liner in place and it can be mortared for stability and permanence.

Limestone is the most popular flagstone. Its appearance improves as it weathers and as moss and algae grow on it. To edge a pool with flagstone, dig a shallow shelf around the pool. Then, experiment with placing the pieces so they fit together neatly. Cut large stones with a circular saw that has a masonry blade, or rent a stone-cutting saw. Wear safety goggles. Local stone is the least expensive and blends most naturally into the landscape.

Brick and concrete pavers

Brick and concrete pavers make great extensions of materials used in patios, walks, or other hardscaping. Depending on the method you use, brick and concrete pavers can be easy to install or they can be a challenge. It's fairly easy to lay them dry in sand, for example, but more difficult to set pavers in concrete.

Mortared brick and pavers have some advantages over those that are set dry. First, you can cantilever them over the water to minimize the amount of exposed liner. Second, mortar won't readily erode into the pond, unlike sand, soil, and other dry construction materials.

Cut stone

More expensive and more formal than flagstone in appearance, cut stone looks most appropriate around square or rectangular pools. Excellent in most formal gardens, it blends well (depending on its color) with gravel, wood, and brick, as well as a number of other materials.

Cut stone is challenging to work with—its right-angled edges must fit perfectly, and it needs to be mortared in place. Cut stone is excellent for cantilevering to conceal the liner. Choose stone with a rough surface so that it won't be too slippery when wet.

◄ **Concrete pavers anchor this circular pond into the paved area behind it.**

▼ **Cut-stone edging is a perfect choice for formal designs such as the circular pool below.**

Boulders

Ideal for naturalistic ponds, small boulders are relatively easy to work with. You'll need help to move any large boulders you install, and unless you find a free supply, their price and delivery costs will be high.

Boulders work well set in sand or gravel, although you can mortar them for permanence. Most boulders should be buried to one-third or one-half of their overall height for a natural effect. Boulders are striking when they are combined with cut stone and flagstone.

▲ **Water features in decks are an easy retrofit. Simply cut into the existing structure, and a flat, possibly boring space becomes a peaceful retreat.**

◄ **Boulders edge this stream and waterfall, making it look natural.**

Patios and decking

Water features built into a patio or deck put the water at a level where it's easy to enjoy. And garden ponds are an easy retrofit—especially to a deck. Cut them into the existing structure or set them adjacent to it.

You won't have to buy separate edging material, so the project will be relatively inexpensive. Make sure that the wood has not been treated with preservatives that can leach into the water and harm plants or fish. And if you're thinking about using redwood, you'll need to season it for at least a year or until it turns gray. Fresh redwood contains toxic tannins.

FOUNTAINS: PLANNING

◄ **Look for a fountain that reflects the garden's personality. This traditional style fountain would not work in a modern landscape.**

HINT

If you want to include fish in your fountain, avoid materials that include lead, which is toxic.

► **This three-tiered, very formal fountain is the focal point of this classic old-world courtyard.**

Most fountains are made of precast concrete. Reconstituted stone and fiberglass have also become popular, simulating the look of stone with amazing realism. Whether concrete or stone look-alike, fountains come in numerous colors and surface finishes. Finding just the right fountain for your garden takes some research. Visit garden centers to scout their offerings. Ask if there are other fountains that you can special order. Also check out mail-order catalogs. If you want a special, one-of-a-kind fountain, visit art fairs or ask at art galleries for the names of local artists who might design a fountain for you.

Wall fountains

Wall fountains, which take up no floor room, are ideal for gardens or seating areas tight on space. Most are powered by a submersible pump that recirculates water from the basin through a delivery pipe up to the spout. The number of designs is nearly infinite, but most have a jet of water spilling into a trough or basin.

Plumbing some wall fountains can be rather complicated. It often requires piping behind the wall. In other cases, the water lines run on the wall surface and must be disguised with vines or other plants.

A fountain packs a lot of charm into a small space. Whether traditional or contemporary, fountains propel a stream of water through the air and create a cooling effect. They're ideal for up-close viewing, which is why fountains are usually located on a porch, patio, or other sitting area.

A fountain can attach to a wall or stand alone. Some freestanding fountains are designed to rest in—or next to—a pool or pond, while others are water features unto themselves, working well on a deck, patio, or lawn, or tucked into a flowerbed. Tabletop fountains have recently become popular, taking just minutes to set up.

You can choose from a wide variety of styles, colors, materials, and sizes. However, choose a fountain that is in keeping with the overall style of your garden and home. A classical statuary fountain might look out of place in a simple country garden, for example. A wall fountain fashioned of brick and stone or stone look-alike is best set against similarly sturdy masonry— not wood—siding.

However, simple-to-install, preformed kits are now available with only a cord running from them. Consider the ease and cost of installation when buying a wall fountain.

Wall fountains attach in several ways. Heavy stone fountains attach with mortar and are supported with T-blocks (decorative braces that act as brackets). Lighter weight fountain kits come with mounting hardware that is self-supporting.

Freestanding fountains

Appealing because of their ease of installation, freestanding fountains also make ideal focal points for a patio, flowerbed, or lawn. In this type of fountain, a small submersible pump is housed in the lower pedestal, in a hollow base beneath the bowl. Its design should allow easy access to the pump so you can clean and maintain it, usually on a monthly basis.

Statuary fountains

These ornamental fountains can be placed near a pond or pool or in the water feature itself. The statue has a supply pipe on its base. The pipe is connected to the pump with flexible tubing. Large statues must have firm footing. For a fountain on the

▲ The statuary fountain above adds needed height and dimension to the inground pool. It makes a bold statement in front of the brick wall.

WEATHERPROOFING YOUR FOUNTAIN

Take good care of your fountain year-round to greatly prolong its life.

One of the best things you can do for concrete fountains and statuary is to apply a concrete sealer to prevent moisture from getting into the concrete and expanding and cracking it when the water freezes. It's also important to drain the fountain before freezing weather arrives to prevent ice from forming on the pump. Ice can crack pump housings and cause seals to fail. It also can crack basins. If you can, drain the fountain by tipping over the basin. If you can't tip the basin, siphon or pump out the water.

Then, prevent rain, ice, and snow from collecting in the basin by covering the fountain or statuary with a sheet of plastic. Secure the plastic to prevent it from flapping in the wind and ripping.

Many pumps can dry out, shrinking the seals and preventing the fountain from working properly. Overwinter your pump in a bucket of water or sealed plastic bag in a basement or heated garage. It's also important that the cord does not dry out; cracked cords can cause dangerous shorts.

---

side of a pond, make sure its resting place (including any edging) is firm and level.

If you want to install the fountain in the pond, you can mount it on a hollow in-pond pedestal created specifically for that purpose or build your own with mortared bricks or stone. If the statue is small, a black plastic storage crate makes an easy, hard-to-detect base as long as the base of the fountain is slightly underwater.

Fountain care

Fountains in sunny spots tend to have problems with algae. If you are not raising fish or plants in your fountain, you can prevent algae by adding chlorine tablets or chlorine bleach to the fountain water. Follow label directions for tablets or add bleach at the rate of 2 ounces of bleach to every 10 gallons of water, once a month. If that doesn't work, increase the amount of bleach to 5 ounces. If you do have plants or fish, consider using an algicide. Make sure it's labeled for use in ponds with fish and plants; follow package directions exactly.

FOUNTAINS: INSTALLING

Depending upon the design of your fountain, installation can take just minutes—or as long as a day or more, even with professional help. Here are the basics.

Wall fountains

Your wall must be sturdy enough to hold the fountain, its basin, and the water it contains. Most wood-sided walls are not strong enough, but many stucco and brick walls are. Check with a contractor or mason if you're unsure of the wall's stability. You may need to include a decorative T-block fitted to the wall as a bracket to support the weight of the basin.

If the plumbing is to be installed through the wall, you'll need to drill holes with a power drill (and masonry bit for stone walls). Drill one hole up high (usually just

▲ If you can't drill through a wall to install a fountain, use surface-mounting hardware.

below eye level) for the water outlet and drill another one low for the water intake. Insert pipe through each hole and join them behind the wall with two elbow joints and a length of flexible pipe.

If the pipe cannot be installed through a wall, you will need to attach it to the surface of the wall. You can chisel a channel into a solid concrete surface to set the pipe flush, but if chiseling will affect the strength of the material (brick or concrete block, for example), use rigid pipe attached to the wall with clamps. Either way, the exterior plumbing must ultimately be disguised with vines or other plants.

Attach the fountain to the wall, usually with a combination of mortar and wall plugs. Connect the pump—if it's not built in—to the intake pipe and plug it into a GFI outlet.

Freestanding fountains

Most freestanding fountains come preplumbed and installation is simple. Check the level of the site on which the fountain will rest and make necessary adjustments to even it up.

Position the fountain and again check its level. If you need to adjust the level, use sand, soil, or bits of stone. Fill the fountain and plug it in (to a GFI outlet only). Order the fountain with a cord long enough to reach the outlet. If the cord doesn't reach the outlet, plug in an extension cord to a waterproof junction box designed specifically for outdoor use.

WALL FOUNTAIN

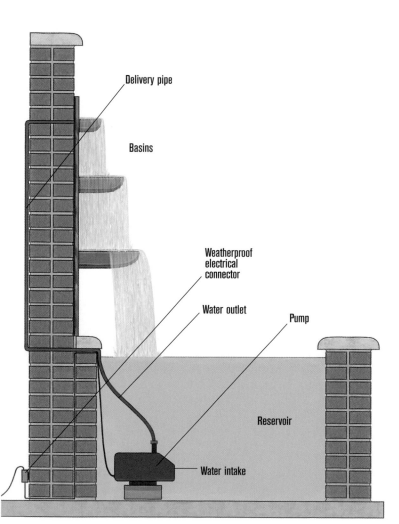

Delivery pipe

Basins

Weatherproof electrical connector

Water outlet

Pump

Reservoir

Water intake

POSITIONING OUT-OF-POOL STATUARY FOUNTAINS

Out-of-pool fountains are an excellent, easy way to add the sound of splashing water to your water garden. These fountains also tie in with the rest of the landscape, and because they're decorative, they add an element of garden art.

Test the position of your out-of-pond fountain by first hooking up the pump and plugging in the fountain. The spray will vary with the design of the fountain but can be made larger or smaller by turning the flow adjuster on the pump. Experiment with placement of the fountain and the power of the flow until you get a pleasing effect. Most out-of-pond fountains look best when set asymmetrically to one side of the water feature.

▶ Out-of-pool statuary fountains add an element of garden art. Experiment with the placement and the power of the flow until you achieve just the effect you want.

Statuary fountains

Most statuary fountains are designed for either in-pond or out-of-pond installation, but some can be used in both locations. Where you position your statuary fountain, therefore, depends primarily on its design.

■ **Out-of-pond fountains:** Small out-of-pond statuary fountains can rest on stones on the edge of the pool or stream. Larger out-of-pond fountains need a more substantial base, such as a perfectly level stone or concrete pad. With both, a pump rests in the pond, recirculating water through a flexible tube. You'll need to disguise the tubing and the electrical cord with stone, plants, or soil.

■ **In-pond fountains:** In-pond statuary fountains are usually larger than out-of-pond models. For that reason, they need a solid foundation on which to rest.

Set small fountains weighing less than 30 pounds on a stack of bricks or cement blocks. For larger fountains, either build a substantial base from mortared brick or stone, or install a precast concrete pedestal for the foundation. If you're building your own base, be sure to allow a core for any piping that will be connected to the pump (most larger fountains are run by an external pump).

Very large statuary—those more than 100 pounds—require footings. Pour at least 6 inches of reinforced concrete in the ground underneath the fountain before installing underlayment and the liner. Then build or install the pedestal on this footing. Cushion the liner with old carpeting.

FREESTANDING FOUNTAIN

HINT

Before you install your in-pond pedestal, put an extra layer of liner under the pedestal base to prevent tears and leaks.

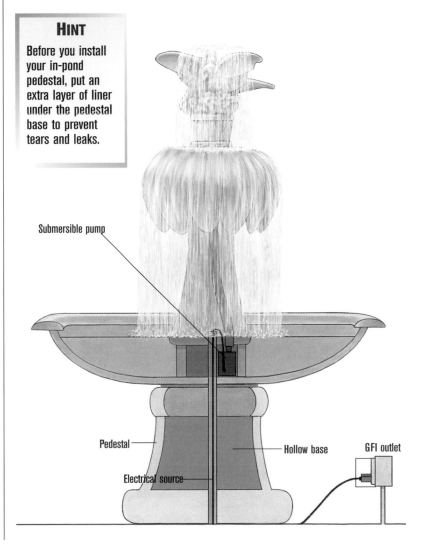

Submersible pump

Pedestal

Electrical source

Hollow base

GFI outlet

STREAMS AND WATERFALLS

▲ **Rocks and stones disguise the liner and mechanics of this watercourse. Give plants, such as water lilies, enough room so their leaves don't get splashed. Many plants with floating leaves also do not like rapidly flowing water.**

You can build streams and waterfalls with the help of modern liner and high-quality pumps. A stream can be just a few feet in length or traverse hundreds of feet. It can include ponds and waterfalls in its course or none at all. A waterfall can be as small as a trickle of water tumbling a few inches over the lip of a stone or as dramatic as a cascade dropping several feet.

Planning a stream

Before designing your stream, study natural creeks and brooks. Take a walk in one of your state parks or take digital photos of water gardens that include streams. Watch how a stream cuts its course, how the banks are formed, where rocks lie, and how plants grow. Note, too, how falls and pools occur. Then take your cue from nature to build your watercourse. Naturalizing a stream is the key to making it look like it was always part of the landscape.

■ **Sketch it out on paper:** Plan your stream on paper first. Make rough and then refined sketches of your design, after you've studied the contours of your landscape.

You can locate a stream just about anywhere in your yard. If your yard has a slope, it will be easy to turn it into a watercourse. However, even if your yard is flat, you can build a slope with infill soil or soil left after digging a pond. You will need only a slight incline (1–2 inches for every 10 feet) to keep the water flowing.

The length of the stream will be your first consideration, and of course, no rules apply here, except those that govern your landscape and the limitations of your budget. If, however, your plans include a pond, the total stream length should be twice the length of any ponds so the features are in scale with each other.

Next, decide on the width for the stream. In general, the wider the stream bed, the more leisurely its current; the narrower, the faster the current. The speed of the current, however, can also be determined by the size of your pump. You can have a rapidly flowing stream in a wide bed, for example, if your plans—and budget—allow for a large pump.

Keep it natural looking

The stream will look more natural if you include a series of short, almost-level sections in the streambed. These sections should be level enough to hold some water even when the pump is off. Connect the sections by drop-offs of just an inch or so.

Add whatever twists and turns you can to the stream. Meandering streams look natural; so do streams with rocks and boulders. Large rocks inside the watercourse create rivulets by diverting water around them. Smaller rocks and pebbles produce ripples as the water moves over them.

■ **Bogs are a good transition:** Mini bogs along the stream will also give the impression that the stream was formed by nature, and you should include them in your sketches. Mini bogs are shallow areas—unconnected to the stream—that you dig (and line) a few feet out from the stream. Bogs are the perfect place for moisture-loving plants. They look (and work) best with rocked and mortared edges and should be filled with water that is independent of the stream. (Don't divert water from the stream; that interferes with its water flow.)

You might want to include a permanent irrigation system to keep the bogs wet. A spaghetti line from your drip irrigation system or a sprinkler will work, but you can water them by hand, as well. Just make sure you water often enough.

Once your sketch is complete, take your design outside. Mark out the watercourse with a hose or rope.

Planning a waterfall

There is no rule on how many waterfalls you should have. A watercourse can have no falls or can be nothing but falls. The height and width of the falls are also entirely up to you.

However, there is one rule you should follow when planning waterfalls: Keep them in scale with the ponds (called catch basins) they empty into. A small trickle will be lost emptying into a large pond and will have little value in circulating and oxygenating the water. On the other hand, a waterfall gushing into a small catch basin will disrupt the surface and stir up sediment, creating poor conditions for fish and plants.

Every waterfall starts with a header pool, a 10-inch (or deeper) pool at the top, or a waterfall tank with a weir opening. The waterfall tank can double as a biofilter. Header pools create a more natural look than water simply spilling from an outlet pipe. Include them in your sketches, and remember that if you'd like a series of waterfalls, the catch basin of one is the header pool for the next.

While you're planning, think about what type of falls you want: a smooth, broad, unbroken curtain of water or a narrow, frothy cascade. The surface of the spill stone (the stone that forms the lip of the fall) determines the way the water falls. For a curtain of water, use a smooth, flat stone. For a frothy cascade, find a spill stone with ridges and bumps, one that funnels water somewhat to its center. Note these on your plans. In a series, you may want a different effect in each waterfall.

When all your plans are completed, mark out the watercourse and waterfall with rope or a hose. Leave it for a day or two before you dig to see if you like what you've designed. Then mark the course in further detail with marker stakes on both sides, every foot or so.

■ **Building a berm:** If you're building up the surface with a berm, put the stakes at the outside edges of the planned berm location, with their tops at the height of the soil you will add. Tie a piece of string between them so you can see the height and contour of your watercourse and waterfalls. Once you've brought in soil, tamp it or let it settle—three months is best. It's important to allow the soil to get packed down before you start digging so it doesn't slide down or settle unevenly after the project is built.

◀ This short waterfall flows into a catch basin filled with gravel and rocks. The gravel affects the sound and the rocks break up the flow, making it look more natural.

HINT

When planning your stream or waterfall, look through nature and outdoor living magazines for ideas on how to incorporate streams and waterfalls into your own landscape. Collect photos to help you plan.

◀ Bog plants line the banks of this rather long watercourse, serving to soften the edges and root the feature in the landscape.

Excavation

The first step in building a stream or waterfall is excavation. If you have an existing slope or hill, its overall incline will largely determine the pitch of your water feature. But if you're creating a watercourse on relatively flat land or if you want a waterfall with substantial heights, you'll need to build a berm with infill soil. The illustrations on this page and on pages 78 and 79 show the details found in streams and waterfalls.

Whether your stream or waterfall will be on a natural incline or a prepared berm, start by refining the layout on your lawn. Move the stakes and twine along the stream sides as you define exactly where your stream will twist and turn. Once you've finalized the course, tie twine from stake to stake at ground level for areas you'll excavate, and above ground level at the height of the areas to be built up. Also, tie a level line—it attaches to the twine with built-in hooks—across the bed at these locations. Your stakeout and twining now will tell you exactly where to dig and where (and how much) soil should be added.

■ **Dig the pool first:** Dig the pond(s), and any catch basin(s), and header pool(s) first (see pages 50 and 51). Move the excavated soil to locations that need fill, or set it aside on tarps for disposal.

Leave a strip—6 inches–1 foot wide— around each pool for rocks and edging. If the header pool is large or if you'll be using very large stones, this edge should actually be a ledge—a foot or more wide and roughly half as deep as the diameter of the boulders—cut around the outside of the pools. If you want bogs along the watercourse, dig them out as well, and make an edge for their borders, too.

■ **Dig the streambed:** Remember that a streambed needs a drop of at least 1–2 inches every 10 feet to ensure a downhill flow, but beyond that, it can be as steep or as gentle as you want.

Excavate the existing ground (or berm if you've brought in fill) to the depth you've chosen for the entire watercourse, using the level to chart the slope of the streambed. On a natural slope, dig to the same depth throughout, checking the incline of the bed frequently. In areas within the stream that will be planted, leave level terraces to ensure that plants and other stream life will stay healthy even if the pump breaks down.

■ **Dig a channel for utilities:** Finally, dig out a channel (about 6 inches deep) outside the liner area in which to lay the piping that will return the water from the pond or foot of the stream to its head. Leave a length of tubing exposed at each end for the inlet and outlet. Trench another channel for electric line conduit.

HINT

Dig stream and catch basins a little larger than you think you want them to be. Once you install edging and stones, they'll look smaller.

ANATOMY OF A STREAM WITH WATERFALLS

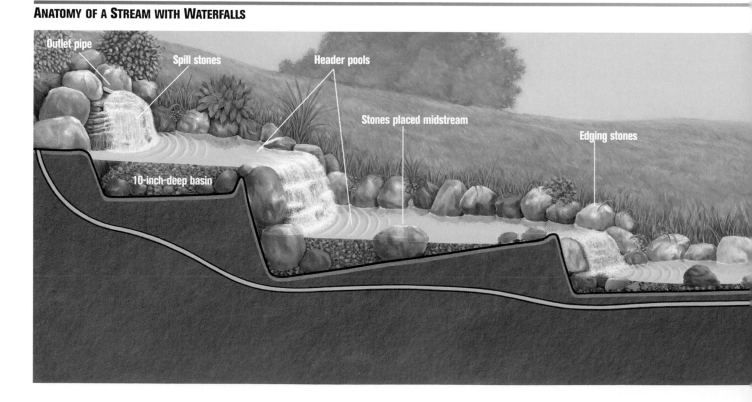

Outlet pipe

Spill stones

Header pools

Stones placed midstream

Edging stones

10-inch-deep basin

Underlayment and liner

Once the watercourse is excavated, cover it with underlayment to shield the liner against punctures. Spread a ½- to 2-inch layer of sand, old carpet, or underlayment. Following the directions on page 56, fit the liner to the excavation. If a single piece of liner can cover the streambed, merely make adjustments as when laying liner in a pool.

■ **Seal liner:** Most likely the stream will require more than one section of liner. If so, overlap the sections. Start at the bottom of the watercourse. Allow for liner to extend from one section into the next (up and over the lip of a waterfall, for example). Lap each upper section over the lower piece. Seal the seams with adhesive or tape made for this purpose. Sealing allows water to flow over the seam and prevents seepage.

Install the pump: trial run

After laying the liner completely in the watercourse, place the pump in the lowest part of the stream, setting it on bricks so it won't take in silt, or use a solid-handling pump. It should be close to the waterfall, if you have built one. In this spot, the pump provides maximum circulation and aeration with the least length of line. Attach the pump to the supply and outlet lines. Now you're ready for a trial run.

SOUND

You can control the sound of your watercourse by the way you create waterfalls and strategically position stones.

Part of what affects sound is the water's speed and volume. Large amounts of water moving rapidly produce a gushing sound. A small rivulet moving slowly sounds more like a ripple. Although pleasant if adjusted properly, a ripple that's too weak can sound like a leaky faucet. Fine-tune the sound of your watercourse by turning the flow valve on the pump.

The more falls you design into the watercourse, the louder the sound. And different types of falls create different sounds. A flat fall where water sheets over the edge makes a subtle—even peaceful—sound. A fall where water cascades down the rocks makes quite a splash. Positioning stones behind the falls creates a hollow space that amplifies and echoes sound.

Placing large stones in the stream not only makes the stream look more natural, it also increases the splashing sound. Add, move, or remove large stones until the stream or waterfall sounds just the way you want it.

Turn on the pump to move water through the course. As the header pools and catch basins fill, fit the liner into place. Fill the pool halfway, readjust the liner, and then fill completely. Make sure that no liner will show after the edging is installed, adding or removing soil beneath the liner to bring the edge level with the water. If you trim the liner, leave enough to go under edging. Make the final trim after the stones are set in place.

Flexible tubing

Flexible liner

Pond

Pump

STREAM AND WATERFALL MATERIALS

GRAVEL AND PEBBLES

Use these as a bottom layer, in conjunction with sand, to cover the liner and to create a gravel bed like those found in nature. Pea gravel is widely available, but check out gravel and pebbles from local quarries. As a rule, darker gravel or pebbles create a more striking look. Avoid brightly colored or white gravel, which looks artificial. Generally, the larger the rock the less prone it is to collecting algae and silt. Gravel is very prone to algae growth; an assortment of larger stones in the floor of the stream is less likely to create a problem.

ROCKS AND STONE

Excellent for edging material, medium-sized rocks and stones can hold down the liner, accent the stream as well as edge it, create a waterfall, and serve many other functions. Choose rocks and stones that look as though they might occur together in nature. Avoid wide contrasts in color such as black lava rock next to limestone. Flat flagstone is invaluable for edging. The more worn and weathered the stone, the more natural it looks.

BOULDERS

Unless you live in a very rocky part of the country, the size of boulders and their expense will mean they can be used only as accents. However, boulders add drama, especially at lower or upper sections of a stream or in a strategic spot that highlights a particularly pretty part of a watercourse. For a natural appearance, partially bury boulders so that one- to two-thirds of their surface is visible. If they're in the water, no more than half of their height should be above water.

Set very large boulders on a concrete footing. Cover the footing with a layer of underlayment, then with the liner and carpet or extra layers of liner to cushion the liner. Next, place the boulder on the footing. If you don't set boulders on such a strong footing, they may settle lower than you want.

Edging and positioning stone

Once the watercourse is lined and the water flow tested, it's time to install the edging. Edging holds the liner in place as well as disguises it. It also helps create a transition from the stream to the surrounding area and makes the watercourse look like it's always been there.

Edging stones can be flat or round and laid in 1–3 courses or—depending on the contours of the landscape—at random: one course at one location, three at another.

You can set edging stones loosely or mortar them in place. Mortaring isn't required, but it prevents water from flowing under the edging, which increases the water feature's volume without requiring a bigger pump.

■ **Position edging stones:** Start by placing edging stones along the inside and outside edge of the entire watercourse, including the streambed, ponds, and mini bogs. You'll probably need to position each rock at least a couple of times to get just the right effect.

■ **Build spillways:** Next, build the spillways for waterfalls, if the water feature has them. Lay flat rocks or other materials to form

HINT

If you notice an unusual drop in the pond level, you may have a leak. To determine whether the leak is in the pond, in the stream, or in the waterfall, turn off the pump. If the level in the pond stays constant, the leak is in the stream or waterfall.

each lip. The top surface of the rocks should be slightly below the water level of the stream or header pool that precedes it. That way, water will flow from the header pool to the catch basin without overflowing the banks.

If the lip will be more than a foot or so across, set a foundation stone vertically under the lip stone. You can also lay stones in the header pool just before the lip, in addition to those you've put in place for edging to form channels to direct water to the falls.

Periodically turn on the pump, or use a hose to test the flow and effect of the water, making sure it moves over the falls the way you want. Change lip stones until you're satisfied with the flow.

■ **Mortar the edging:** Once the edging and spillways are in place, trim off excess liner. If you're not mortaring, pat good-quality soil in nooks among the stones to make pockets for plants. Mortared edging and spillways are more difficult. After you experiment with the stones to get the right arrangement, mortar them in sections. Take out the stones, lay the mortar bed, and then replace the stones. Fill in between stones with mortar. Be careful not to use so much mortar that it detracts from the natural look of the edging.

Use bagged mortar mix, or mix your own with 1 part lime, 2 parts portland cement, and 9 parts sharp sand. To help the mortar blend in, add a mortar dye that matches the general color of the stone. After the mortar dries, treat it with household vinegar or muriatic acid to cure it and keep it from leaching lime. Lime increases the water pH, which is potentially toxic to fish. Follow label directions and wear protective gear—muriatic acid is extremely dangerous. After treating the mortar, rinse all concrete surfaces thoroughly to remove acid residue. Do not allow the rinse water to remain in any part of the water feature; muriatic acid is deadly to fish and plants.

PREFORMED WATERFALLS

Rigid units provide a relatively easy way to create a small waterfall, and usually include all the materials (except for the pump) that you need. Rigid units, however, are significantly less natural looking than falls made with flexible liner. Plants that drape over the edge of the unit can help it blend into the landscape. Some rigid waterfalls are available in formal styles, but are difficult to find outside of Europe.

Preformed rigid waterfall units come in a variety of finishes, forms, and materials. Some have a natural shape, while others are boldly modern. Most are made of molded plastic or PVC. The units are manufactured as either one-piece models or in designs with several parts that require friction-fit or bolted assembly.

To install a preformed waterfall unit inground, first mark its outline on the ground and dig a shallow trench with a backward slope into the berm or hill to match the outline. Set the bottom piece (or the entire waterfall of a one-piece unit) in a bed of sifted soil or a mix of fine soil and moist sand. Working from the lowest point to the highest, backfill with the soil/sand mixture. Position each subsequent section, overlapping the section below it and continuing to backfill. Install aboveground units on sturdy bases.

Hide the lower portion of the delivery pipe in a shallow trench alongside the unit. Use a flat rock, plant, or other item to conceal the top of the delivery pipe. For the most natural effect, arrange additional stones around the unit, perhaps scattering some randomly along its edges. Turn on the water and adjust the flow valve to get the right effect. Rigid units usually do best with a very gentle flow.

INSTALLING A STREAM

1 If necessary, create a berm to give the watercourse the necessary slope. Compact any infill soil or let it settle for three months. Mark out the watercourse with stakes and twine. Then begin digging, creating any preplanned pools first, then the stretches of stream.

2 Install underlayment to prevent tears in the liner. Spread out the flexible liner, positioning and folding it as needed. For larger streams, overlap the higher sections on each lower one. Position the seam at a waterfall rather than in a runway. Seal the seam.

3 Position the pump in the pond at the opposite end from the waterfall or stream, where it will provide maximum water aeration. Attach the pump to piping in the pond and run it up along the stream to the outlet that you've roughly positioned into place.

4 Turn on the pump and check to see how the water flows down the course. Make any necessary adjustments by adding or removing soil under the liner.

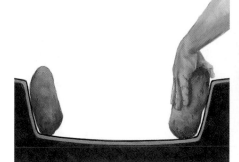

5 Lay a rough row of stones along the stream edges. You can mortar the stones or foam them into place to prevent water from flowing under them and being wasted. Cut off excess foam after it dries.

6 Disguise the liner with small stones, pebbles, and gravel in the bed. Scatter some among the edging stones, too, for a natural effect. Use as little gravel as possible because it tends to collect and promote algae. Retest the flow.

7 With the pump running, experiment with the placement of larger stones to see how they affect sounds and the splashing effect. Add or subtract stones as needed or reposition existing stones. Trim liner edges.

Laying stones in the bed

After laying the edging around the watercourse, the next step is to disguise the liner with bed stones. These are rocks of mixed shapes and sizes that you place on the floor of the stream.

Once you've laid the main bed with small stones, experiment with the position of larger stones. Larger rocks help to hide the liner and help to add splash, sparkle, and movement to the stream when they are placed where the current flows over and around them. Use rocks in a variety of shapes and sizes, referring to personal photographs or pictures of streams you've clipped from magazines as you planned your water feature.

Next, position the water outlet or waterfall box in its permanent location above the top header pool. Disguise it with rocks, soil, and plants. Conceal any piping along the watercourse by burying it under soil or stones.

If a lot of soil or debris has collected in the pond and watercourse as you worked—or if you used vinegar or muriatic acid to clean the pond—empty the watercourse by either pumping or bailing. Rinse out any remaining acid or debris. Then completely refill it with fresh water.

You can further refine the flow of the water along the watercourse—making it run faster or slower—by adjusting the flow valve on the pump, if available, to achieve the desired rate of flow through the stream.

HOW TO CREATE A WATERFALL

A waterfall can be a small splash down a few rocks into a tiny trough or a trickle on the side of a pond, or it can be a huge, roaring cascade as part of an extensive stream. A waterfall can work alone or as one of several in a series.

A waterfall that is part of a stream has essentially three parts: the header pool, the lip over which water falls, and the catch basin. Water collects in the header pool then spills over the lip and into the catch basin (which can be a header pool for the next waterfall, if there is one).

When digging a waterfall, create a 12-inch shelf of compacted soil that extends into the streambed to support the weight of the waterfall lip and any stones on it. You can also support the lip with boulders, concrete blocks, bricks, packed mortar, or poured concrete. Install underlayment and liner over the support.

Waterfalls made with larger rocks—a foot or more across—look more natural and are more stable if you prop the lip on a foundation stone: a rectangular piece (or two) set vertically under the lip.

Mini waterfalls have become popular as more gardeners seek small-space features for their landscape. These designs are very small, taking up less space than a bread box. You can build them to stand independently in the landscape or position them alongside a pool or pond. However they're designed, they create a charming way to add splash and a cooling effect to your landscape.

To create a mini waterfall on the side of a pool or pond, install flexible piping on the pump. Run the piping to the intended site for the waterfall and arrange a pile of stones 1 or 2 feet high (you may want to build up a small earth mound on which to position them). You can create a lip and foundation stone for the waterfall or you can arrange the stones in any other manner. Turn the pump on periodically to see how the water flows over the stones. The entire waterfall must be underlayed with flexible liner overlapping the pool's liner, and seamed with sealant or tape to contain the water.

You may want to purchase a preformed mini-waterfall unit. Install it at the side of the pool or pond with its lip slightly overlapping the edge of the pool, then pack loose soil and sand around it. Run the plumbing the same way you would for a stone waterfall.

▲ Create a mini waterfall by laying stones in a "pile." Position one rock, such as this large flat stone, to serve as the waterfall's lip.

▲ Build up the pile further and position flexible tubing attached to a submersible pump in the pond. Adjust the flow to get just the right effect.

PLANTING & STOCKING A GARDEN POOL

Plants and fish put the crowning touches on a water garden. They add greenery, color, and animation to even the smallest and simplest of water features.

First-time water gardeners will be amazed at how quickly a whole new world can grow, literally at their feet—fascinating water plants send roots below the pond surface, exotic lilies float leisurely along the water, fish with elegant, ribbonlike fins dart among the depths.

If you're a beginning water gardener, you should start with small plants and inexpensive mosquito fish during the first year or two until you become more experienced in managing your water garden. That way, if something dies, you've lost little time and money.

Whether you're a novice or expert, climate partly determines which plants and

fish you can have. Cold-climate gardeners, for example, must make special provisions for tender plants, such as tropical water lilies, and for overwintering fish.

Planning is the key to plant and fish selection. You don't have to chart everything in detail, but when selecting water-garden plants, make a list with an eye for variety—textures, shapes, heights, and colors—just as you would in the landscape at large. Select a mix of floating plants, those that grow in shallow water, and deep-water plants. Look for some with narrow, upright-growing foliage to add height to your water garden, and include others with bold texture for emphasis. Take into consideration plant sizes at maturity (they might grow larger than you think), as well as how aggressive a plant might be—a problem especially pronounced in some water plants.

CHOOSING PLANTS

Water lilies and other deep-water plants: Rooted in pots at the bottom of the pond, water lilies and their cousins, lotuses, send up leaves that float on the surface. They shade the water and keep it cool. There are two kinds of water lilies: tropical and hardy. Tropical water lilies grow from bulbs and are profuse bloomers with blossoms that stand on stems above the water surface. Hardy water lilies grow from tubers and are somewhat less showy. Their blossoms are smaller and most float on the water surface. Wait until the water has warmed to 60°F before you plant tropical water lilies. Plant hardy varieties when the ice is off the pond. To learn more about caring for water lilies and lotuses, see pages 84 and 85.

Submerged plants: Submerged plants, such as water milfoil and hornwort, also grow in pots at the bottom of the pond, but their foliage grows primarily or completely underwater. They are often called oxygenators, and some do, in fact, add small amounts of oxygen to the water. They also absorb carbon dioxide and minerals, which inhibit algae growth. Submerged plants provide underwater cover—good spawning areas for fish— and some provide food for the fish as well. They also help filter the water. Submerged plants are sold in bunches of six stems. Plant one bunch about every 1–2 square feet. Submerged plants need less soil than water lilies and require a higher proportion of sand or gravel. Don't fertilize submerged plants; they get their nutrients from minerals dissolved in the pond. Mix varieties; some will do better than others.

▲ **Floating plants (foreground) should be placed away from moving water.**

▼ **Water lilies are beautiful deep-water plants that, on their own, provide ample reason to create a water garden.**

Selecting plants for your first water garden might seem daunting. But the unknown is a challenge and exciting. Here's some useful information to get you started.

There are five types of water-garden plants. Refer to the Gallery of Plants, which starts on page 96, to make your choices. Experiment with one type or try all five types of water gardens. However, if you examine the healthiest unfiltered water gardens, you'll probably find that those with the cleanest water have a balanced mix of floating plants, submerged plants, and deep-water aquatics.

Floating plants: As the name implies, these float in the water—their leaves and blossoms on the surface, their roots dangling loose beneath. The floating plant group, which includes water lettuce, water hyacinth, and duckweed, provides shade and, often, food for fish or wildlife. Some species are natural water filters. Ideally, the foliage of floaters and other deep-water plants should cover about half of the pond surface to shade the water. If the plants cover more than two-thirds of the pond, they trap carbon dioxide and other dangerous gases in the water. Floaters are easy to grow and maintain: Set the plants in the water, and they take care of themselves. If they get out of control, simply pull them out by hand.

■ **Marginals:** These are shallow-water plants grown in pots on shelves at the edge of the garden pond. They thrive in standing water. Many, such as iris and arrowhead, can double as bog plants. In the water, they're best grown in containers that you can lift for grooming and dividing. That will prevent them from becoming invasive.

Marginal plants act as excellent natural filters in a waterfall or at pond's edge. They also add color and form and help disguise the hard edge of the pond. You may want to try putting several plants of one marginal in one large container, but don't mix species in a pot—the stronger-growing ones will overtake the weaker.

■ **Bog plants:** Bogs are areas where the water table is high, but the plants may not constantly be in standing water. Bog plants grow in heavy soil. In addition to easing the transition from pond to dry land, bog gardens act as a large natural filter. Bog gardens attract a variety of wildlife. Marsh marigolds, sedges, and hibiscus are among the many choices of bog plants.

Which plants?

When planning for plants, measure the pool's surface area so you can space the plants correctly. Make rough sketches of your prospective garden pond from various angles and include the location of the plants. Try a variety of forms, colors, textures, and bloom times. Include trees and other surrounding plants in your sketches to get an overall impression of the impact of your design.

HINT

In still water, position floating plants around potted marginals. They'll help block the view of the pots to create a more natural-looking pond.

Dry-land garden design principles apply to ponds. You can use a single large plant as a specimen, but smaller plants in groups of three or more will have the strongest effect. Don't overdo it; water should be the focus of your garden pool. Plants should enhance, not dominate.

Before you buy any plant, find out how well behaved it is. Water-garden plants, especially floating plants, have a tendency to be invasive in ideal climates. Some states ban certain water garden species because they clog the natural waterways. Invasive plants also will battle you for control, and you'll spend much time pulling them.

■ **Plants and fish:** Also take into account how fish will interact with your plants. Duckweed, for example, although invasive, is a favorite food for goldfish and koi. The fish will often eat it rapidly and keep it under control. Koi and some other fish are frequently boisterous and will uproot and shred plants.

Water movement is another element to plan for. Deep-water aquatics, especially water lilies and other plants with floating leaves, prefer water that is relatively still. Other plants thrive in fast-moving currents. Still others do well in either. A fountain can push floaters away with its splashing or it may wet their leaves, which many plants don't like.

A perennial plant's hardiness (its ability to survive winter cold) can often be extended by simply lowering it below the expected ice depth in autumn. If you live where winter temperatures reach –10°F, for example, plants hardy to 20°F may thrive if you set them where they will not freeze.

GROWING WATER GARDEN PLANTS

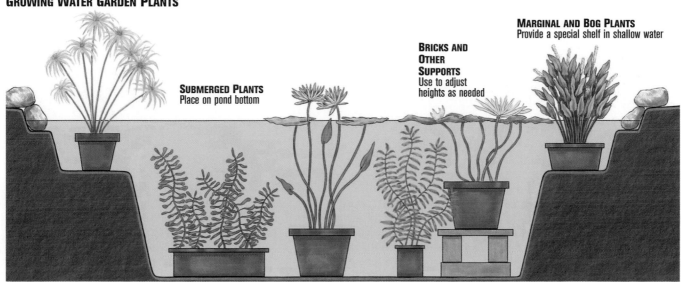

SUBMERGED PLANTS
Place on pond bottom

BRICKS AND OTHER SUPPORTS
Use to adjust heights as needed

MARGINAL AND BOG PLANTS
Provide a special shelf in shallow water

MAINTAINING LILIES AND LOTUSES

Overwintering tropical water lilies

While a lot of people who live north of USDA Hardiness Zone 8 grow tropical water lilies as annuals, with a little effort you can overwinter them, thus saving on buying them each year. In mild climates, you can protect the tropical water lily roots from freezing simply by lowering their tub to the deepest pond section. The exact depth depends on how cold your winters are. Remember, the rootstock must not freeze. Alternatively, prior to the first frost, remove the tropical water lilies from their pots and trim off most of the leaves and roots. Repot them into smaller containers and store in an aquarium tank or other water-filled container where the plants will get plenty of light and where the temperature can be maintained at about 68°F.

If you don't have room to store an entire plant, you can induce it to produce bulbs, and then store the bulbs in airtight containers over the winter. Here's how:

1 Wait until after the first two frosts so the dying foliage can feed the bulbs. When the water temperature drops to about 50°F, remove the pot from the water and dig out the tubers. A viable bulb will be very hard and will sink to the bottom if put in water.

2 Rinse the unearthed bulbs and trim off any roots and stems. Air dry them for a few hours. Store them in covered glass jars or plastic containers buried in damp (not wet) peat, sphagnum moss, or sand. Label the containers with the name of the water lily.

3 Store the bulbs in a dark place where temperatures will stay between 40°F and 60°F and where mice cannot get to them. Check monthly throughout the winter to be sure the bulbs don't dry out, and mist them with water if they have become dry.

4 To get a head start on the season, start your bulbs indoors about 8 weeks before the growing season begins outside. Fill a cup halfway with good topsoil, and then add a layer of sand or pea gravel. Place the bulb so that about half is sitting out of the sand. Fill the cup with water and put it on a heat mat. Once a few leaves have formed, move the cup to a heated aquarium kept between 70°F and 80°F. Give the plant starts lots of light. When the pads grow up to the water's surface and white roots appear, break the new plantlet away from the tuber and plant it. Keep it fertilized and in warm water. When the outdoor water temperature reaches 60°F, replant the bulbs in fresh soil. Put the bulb at the top of the soil surface, pointy side up. Begin with the pot elevated close to the water surface.

DIVIDING OVERGROWN TROPICALS

In climates where tropicals grow year round, they'll outgrow their confines about every two or three years. When you notice that the plant is growing out of the soil, the leaves are smaller and the blooms fewer, it's time to divide and repot. You can do the job in spring or autumn. Follow the directions for hardy water lilies, except the division should be placed vertically in the center of the container, not on its side against the edge.

Dividing hardy water lilies

While your water lily pads are spreading nicely across the surface of your pond, the roots also are growing. Trapped inside the planting container, eventually they'll outgrow their space. Check the containers in spring. If you find tubers that are escaping from their pots, then it's time to divide. In warmer climates where the hardy lilies never go completely dormant, you may need to tackle the job annually. In colder climates with less growing time, lilies may do fine in the same container for 2-3 years. The ideal time to divide water plants is during that in-between time after the danger of freezing has passed, but before the plants start growing too actively.

1 Remove the plant from the container. Wash the soil off, using the strong force of a hose. Cut the tubers apart with a sharp knife. Cut smaller varieties such as 'Perry's Baby Red' to 2-inch lengths; larger varieties such as 'Joey Tomocik' need 5 inches. Cut off new eyes and older leaves, and all but the new, emerging white roots.

2 Fill a 15-inch wide, 10-inch deep container ¾ full with sandy loam soil. Press three fertilizer pellets into the soil. Add a little extra soil against one side of the container, and place the tuber at a slight angle, with the cut edge against the side with extra soil. Add soil until just the growing tip is exposed above the soil. Tamp down the soil and cover it with about 1 inch of pea gravel or grit, keeping the growing tip uncovered.

3 Add water to the container, and then place the plant in shallow water just a few inches below the surface. To adjust the water depth over the pots, use bricks, plant stands or inverted pots as props under the plants to position them. When mature, water lilies should be grown at a depth of 8–12 inches. Fertilize every four to six weeks until August.

Planting lotus

Except for the specially bred dwarf varieties, lotuses are large plants. They spread rampantly, so they are not recommended for earth-bottom ponds, unless you are willing to have them completely take over to a depth of 5 feet. To avoid an invasion, grow the plants in containers. Full-sized lotus varieties need a round planting tub that is at least 18 inches in diameter and 9 inches deep, which is approximately 7–10 gallons of soil. A huge pot 3 feet in diameter and 12 inches deep is even better. Semi-dwarf varieties require a 16×7-inch pot and dwarf or bowl lotus need a 10×6-inch pot. In all cases, the larger the container, the more likelihood the lotus will reach its full blooming potential. To bloom properly, lotuses also require full sun, a minimum of six hours a day.

Plant bare root lotus as early in spring as your climate allows, before the rootstock has sprouted into a tangle of runners. Handle them carefully: the growing buds, called "eyes," can snap off easily.

1 Untangle the mass of roots and rhizomes to find the end of the lotus rhizome. Use caution when handling lotus rhizomes. They are fragile, and damage to the growing tips could kill them. Count back two nodes (joints with roots and buds on rhizome), and cut 1–4 inches behind the second node. You may find several sections to plant. Discard those you don't need, or give them to friends with water gardens.

2 Fill the container to within 2–4 inches from the top with heavy garden soil, mix in 5–10 grams of tablet fertilizer per gallon of soil, and tamp the soil down firmly. Lay the tuber horizontally across the soil in the center of the pot with the growing eye pointing up. Weight down the tuber with a flat stone to keep it from being pushed up when the roots develop, then cover it with additional soil, leaving ½ inch of the tip exposed. Top with a ½-inch layer of pea gravel, keeping it away from the growing bud.

PLANTING AND CARING FOR POTTED WATER PLANTS

▲ **Unless your pond has a clay bottom, you'll need to plant your water garden plants in containers.**

While plants in natural clay ponds root in the mud on the bottom of the pond, those in garden pools (except floating plants) thrive in pots.

Most are potted similar to terrestrial plants and then set gently in the pool. You can introduce them into the pond immediately after filling it, following the precautions on page 23.

Choices for pots are numerous. You can use a regular black plastic pot, which blends into the background. Or, you can use aquatic baskets that have a large open weave. Line these with burlap, landscape fabric, or a woven plastic made for ponds before using.

The size of the container is determined by the needs of the plant. A vigorous water lily, for example, requires a container that's

> **HINT**
> You don't need to use special aquatic containers for planting. Those black plastic pots that regular nursery plants come in are fine—and free.

about 16 inches across. Most marginals can survive in an 8–10-inch pot. Tall plants may need broader pots to keep the wind from tipping them over. Small containers should have ballast—a brick in the bottom of the pot works well.

The number of plants you can fit into a container also depends on the plant. Each lily, for example, should grow in its own basket so its leaves are shown off without competition from other plants. Many submerged plants, on the other hand, do well squeezed four or five in a 10-inch pot. Use your best judgment, but err on the side of too much room in the container.

Pot water garden plants in high-quality topsoil made specifically for water gardens. Don't use potting soils with peat, perlite, or wood; these materials float out of the container (ask the retailer if a brand you're considering contains these ingredients). Peat also increases the acidity of the water. Avoid potting soil that contains fertilizer. After planting, top the soil with pea gravel to hold it down and prevent it from floating out.

Setting the depth

To position plants at the right depth, set their containers on a stack of weathered exterior bricks or landscape pavers, or place them on black plastic storage boxes (buy the milk-crate type with grid or mesh sides so they don't float).

When planting water lilies and other deep-water aquatics, some gardeners immediately place the container at its permanent depth. Others believe deep-water plants do better if they are gradually lowered into the water as they grow so their leaves are always afloat. To pursue the second strategy, remove a brick or two as the stems grow, continuing until the pot rests at the proper depth of about 8 inches.

Easy does it

Placing a container in the center of a large water feature is easy if the plants are in pots with handles. Run twine or rope through the handles, and set the container near the water's edge. Recruit a friend to help, then each of you take an end of the rope and stand on opposite sides of the pond. Lower the plant gently into place on its stand, and pull out the cord.

Tidy up

As your plants grow, trim off any dead or diseased plant matter. Carefully deadhead (cut off) spent flowers to promote continued blooming, to prevent disease, and to keep the water garden tidy. Skim out floaters that cover too much surface area of the pool. Established submerged plants may have to be thinned by raking out the overgrowth every few weeks or, lift the pot and trim off some stems. Net leaves, grass clippings, and other debris every day or so to prevent them from decaying and fouling the water.

Fertilizing and disease

Once established, water garden plants benefit from fertilizing. But regular fertilizers can be toxic to fish and can encourage algae. Use aquatic fertilizer instead; it's sold as large pellets, which you push into the soil. Aquatic fertilizer is available at garden centers or through mail-order companies (see "Garden Pool Resources" on pages 119 and 120).

You can prevent many plant pests (both insects and diseases) by choosing plants suited to your climate, by practicing proper water garden care, and by maintaining a balanced ecosystem. Fish and frogs, for example, are helpful because they eat many insect pests.

The incidence of disease in water plants is small, but when disease does strike, select a product specifically labeled for use in water gardens. Some pesticides throw off the balance of the pond and promote algae and other problems. Others may be toxic to fish.

Division

In your second and subsequent years of water gardening, your plants may crowd their pots or become rampant; if so, they need division. You'll know by the signs: reduced bloom and congested crowns in which older foliage crowds out young stems and leaves. Marginals may show dead roots around the crown. Water lily tubers might overgrow the top of the pot or fill it so tightly they distort its shape.

To divide plants that grow from rhizomes, remove them from their pots and cut each into several pieces. Repot each piece having a growing tip. Plants with runners or plantlets can usually be divided by breaking off the "baby" plant.

PLANTING IN A CONTAINER

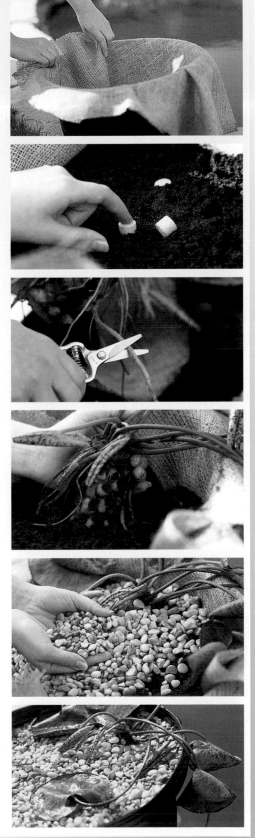

You can plant water garden plants (except floaters) in black plastic pots and place them at various levels of the pool. If using containers made specifically for water planting, line mesh baskets with burlap before filling the pot with soil.

To pot a plant, remove it from its original container. It's a good idea to rinse off the plant. Partially fill the pot with good-quality topsoil (avoid soils containing peat, perlite or wood). If feeding, use only slow-release aquatic fertilizer tablets.

Trim damaged or broken roots. Tropical water lilies should be set in the center of the container, while hardy water lilies should be set at the edge of the pot facing the center. Make sure the plant is at the same level it was in its original container.

Add additional plants if there is room in the container, and fill the pot with soil (to about a half inch below the rim). Now is a good time to pinch off any damaged or yellow leaves.

Spread a layer of pea or dark gravel on top of the soil to keep it from floating out of the container and to help it blend into the background of the pond bottom.

Position the plant in the pond at the correct level. To raise a plant, stack a few weathered bricks underneath it or put the pot on a black plastic storage crate. With some plants, you may need to get into the pool. Wear old tennis shoes or waders.

FISH

Fish add sparkle and movement to a water garden like nothing else. Before you stock your pond, however, there are a number of things to consider.

First, check the water. Ask your supplier what chemicals the water contains. It's likely that it has chloramines. Chloramines must be removed with a chloramine remover. With good circulation you can introduce fish to the water within 20 minutes of adding a chloramine remover. (See page 23 for more information about treating water.)

Climate and conditions

Plan fish purchases with your climate and your pond size in mind. Most fish do best in large ponds because water temperatures and oxygen levels are more stable in larger volumes of water. Some fish do well only in cool water, others prefer warmth, and still others tolerate both extremes.

As a rule, the smaller the pond, the more tolerant of temperature extremes your fish must be. Water heats and cools with ambient temperatures; larger ponds are slower to respond to the changes so the temperature is more consistent. For that reason, a pond that is more than 3 feet deep can house fish with a narrow tolerance for temperature change. But fish in a small pond or container garden with just 50–75 gallons of water, or less, must be able to take extremes of both heat and cold. A half whiskey barrel, for example, is adequate for one or two fish—as long as you choose species that aren't finicky about temperature.

Different fish do best at different depths. Koi, for example, prefer plenty of space in water that is at least 2 feet deep, but orfes spend most of their time in the upper levels of a pond.

The ideal stocking time is late spring or early summer when the water reaches about 50°F. Although you can stock nearly any kind of fish in your pond, those bred for outdoor conditions will require less care and will generally do better in garden ponds than those bred for aquariums.

GALLERY OF FISH

RED-AND-WHITE COMET
A relatively new type of goldfish, red-and-white comets boast elegantly long fins and tail. They feed at all levels and are hardy, tolerating water as cool as 34°F and as warm as 95°F, but not for long at either extreme.

GOLD FANTAIL
Gold fantails are similar to comets but have a more egg-shaped body and an even larger, double tail. Their scales can appear metallic or pearly. Fantails tolerate temperatures of 55°F–70°F. They are sensitive to prolonged low temperatures but less so than calico fantails.

SHUBUNKIN
Often called calico goldfish, shubunkins are popular and easy to care for. They come in many colors, including blue. Several varieties are available, including London, which has a calico pattern on a striking blue background. Bristol shubunkins have the same pattern as Londons, and also have pearly scales and a large forked tail with rounded ends. Shubunkins grow to 10 inches or more and tolerate temperatures between 39°F and 85°F.

KOI
Though choice koi are costly, not all are expensive. They grow to about 2 feet, are hearty eaters, especially of plants, and, if fed, need a large pond with a good filtration system. They can be boisterous enough to knock over pots. Koi feed at all levels and breed easily. They prefer cool temperatures between 39°F and 68°F.

COMMON GOLDFISH
Usually orange-red, the common goldfish feeds at all water levels. Most grow less than 10 inches long, are easily bred, and may live for 10 years or more. They prefer a weedy pond with a muddy bottom. Hardy, they will tolerate water as cool as 39°F and as warm as 95°F, though at neither extreme for long.

What to look for

Most tropical fish centers and water garden nurseries carry a variety of goldfish, koi, and other varieties. Fish vary considerably in appearance, cost, and care. Common goldfish are a favorite and are easy to keep, but more exotic—and more costly—fish are available. There are oranda, which cover their heads with a "hood," and egg-shaped moors with telescopic eyes that protrude from supports. Koi are a favorite of breeders and are even shown in competitions.

If possible, handpick your fish to make sure they're healthy. They should be young, preferably not over 5 inches long, with bright eyes, a sturdy body, and a lively habit. The fish should swim effortlessly with erect fins and have no damaged or missing scales. Choose several small fish instead of a mixture of large and small varieties; small fish (less than 3" long) may become food for larger companions.

Bringing them home

Transport the fish in a plastic bag inside a box. Cover the box so that light won't overheat the bag. If the fish will be in the bag for more than four hours, ask the dealer to add oxygen to the bag. Even with oxygen added, don't leave fish in a sealed bag for more than 36 hours.

Acclimate the fish to the pool by floating the bag on the pool for 10-20 minutes before releasing them. After putting them in the pond, don't feed the fish for the first three or four days. Then, as they settle in, you may feed them daily, but never more than what they can eat in one minute. Excess food will pollute the water. Most fish supplement their diets in the summer with plants, mosquito larvae, and gnats so you can reduce or eliminate summer feedings. If your pond includes plants and koi, start with small fish and avoid feeding them from the outset. This will help prevent them from learning to destructively feed on the plants in your pond. Note: large koi that have learned to feed on plants will train smaller ones to the same behavior.

Fish will need shade and cover in the pool. Provide shade with plants or bricks, stone, and other materials placed on the bottom or shelves of the pond. You should also equip the pond with a UV clarifier.

If your fish are hardy (hardiness varies, but single-tailed varieties are the hardiest), they can overwinter in the deep zone of the pond, which shouldn't freeze. The fish will

HINT

When introducing fish to your pond, treat all the fish in the pond with fish salts to ensure they are disease and parasite free.

live off their fat reserves. All hardy fish can survive temperatures as low as 39°F as long as there is open water at all times for oxygen to enter and gases to escape. An electric deicer will thaw the ice to provide an opening.

Bring tropical fish and fish in pools that freeze solid inside when temperatures drop to 60°F. Keep them in an aerated aquarium or tub. In spring, after water temperatures reach 50°F, reintroduce them to the pond. Resume feeding hardy fish that wintered in the pool.

HOW MANY FISH?

To calculate the number of fish you can have in your garden pool, figure the total surface area of the water feature in which fish will be present. See page 24 for formulas. (This will give you an indication of how much oxygen will be available to them.) Don't count areas with marginal plants in the total but do include the area covered by floating plants.

As a general rule, each inch of fish should have 6 square inches-1 square foot of water. (Koi, however, need more space—about two, 4-5-inch koi per square yard.) Always err on the side of too much space. Use the table below to help you determine the right combination of fish for your pond.

- 2-inch fish: 1 square foot
- 4-inch fish: 2 square feet
- 6-inch fish: 3 square feet
- 8-inch fish: 4 square feet
- 12-inch fish: 6 square feet
- 16-inch fish: 12 square feet

If you provide aeration in the form of a fountain, you can add a few more fish. If you have a waterfall, which aerates and filters the water substantially, you may be able to double the number of fish.

▲ The fish formula: The optimum number of fish is determined by the total volume of the water and the size of the fish.

MAINTAINING YOUR GARDEN POOL

▲ Water lilies like this one look delicate but are actually easy to grow.

A well-designed water garden should take minimal time to maintain. Unless you have a very large water feature, you'll spend about an hour or less each week to feed the fish, groom the plants, and monitor the water quality. When estimating the amount of time to budget for garden pool maintenance, 10 minutes weekly per thousand gallons of water is usually sufficient.

Completely emptying and cleaning the water feature on a regular basis isn't necessary, nor is it advisable. Frequent emptying and cleaning can upset the pond's fragile ecological balance. At most, water gardens need a thorough cleaning only once every three or four years.

If you find that caring for your water garden is taking too much time, it may have a fundamental problem in its design or construction or in the ecological balance of plants, fish, and water. It's better to correct the basic problem instead of spending hours each week fixing its side effects. In the long run, you'll save time and money. If you can't determine the cause of the underlying problem, consider a consultation with a professional water-garden designer.

As long as the pond has no problems, you'll have a burst of chores in the spring and fall and just a little grooming each week in between. The rest of the time is yours—sit back and enjoy the fruits of your hard work.

► This entry bridge crosses a courtyard pond where colorful koi gather for hand-feeding.

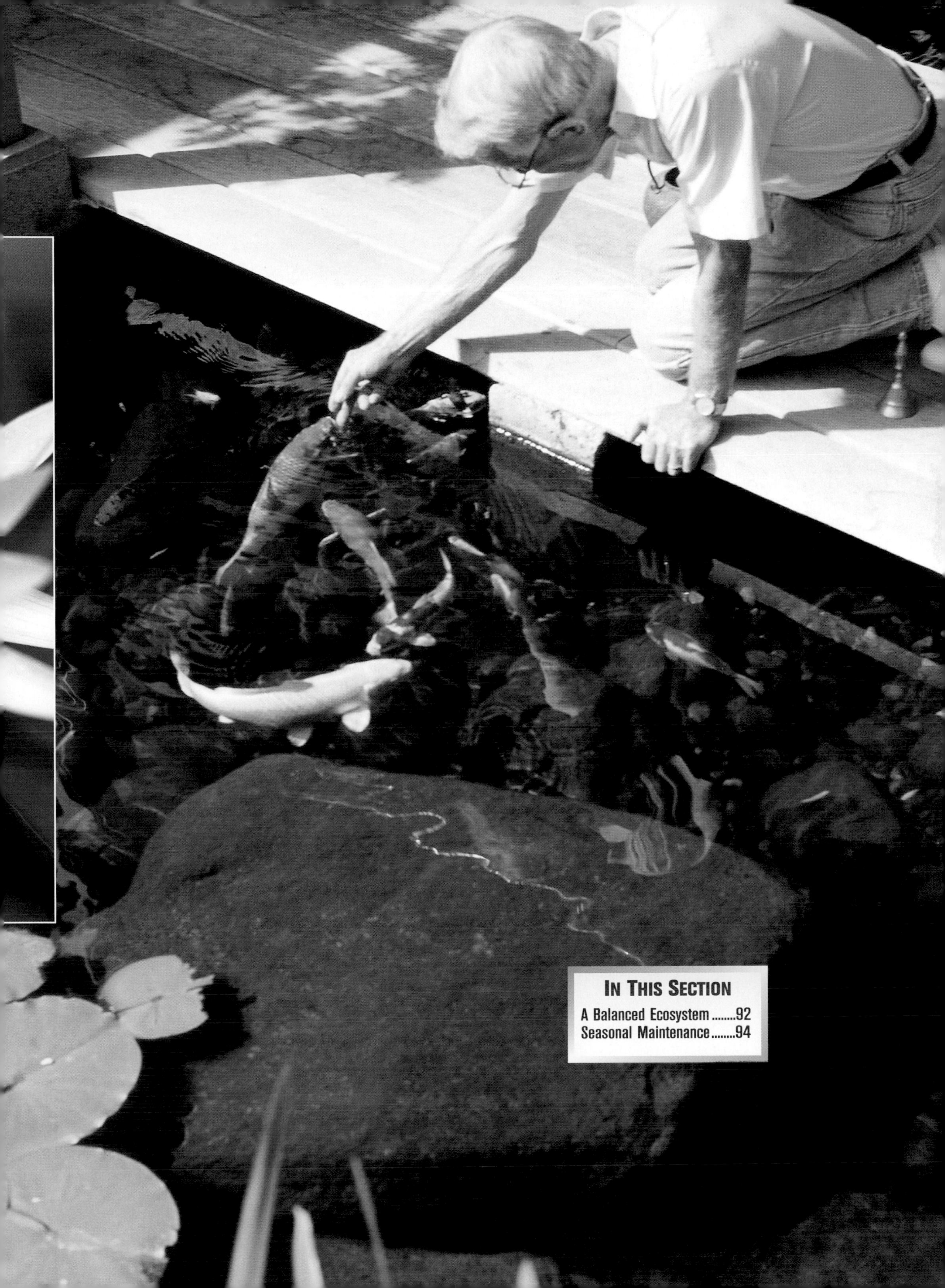

In This Section

A BALANCED ECOSYSTEM

In all but the simplest water features, the clarity of water and the health of the plants and fish depend on a balanced ecosystem. Ponds in the wild and garden pools alike contain a complex network of checks and balances that generally maintain the pond's condition without external help.

If your pond is out of balance, it will give you numerous signals: bad smells, fish dying or gasping for breath at the water surface, dark or green water, as well as stunted and diseased plants.

Keeping the pond balanced

■ **Use all the elements:** Plants, fish, and other pond life—in water that is well-aerated and maintained—work together. All of them, in the right mix, will keep your pond in prime condition.

▼ In a balanced ecosystem such as the one shown here, plants, fish, and other pond life work together to keep the water healthy.

Floating plants provide shade, cool and filter the water, and control algae. Submerged plants are also filters, and they feed fish as well as create shelter and spawning areas. Fish control mosquitoes by consuming the larvae and will feed on algae, too. Snails, also, have voracious appetites for algae.

Stock fish and plants in appropriate proportions to each other and to pond size. Experiment until the balance is right. As a rule, a 6×8-foot pond can handle no more than 16 fish (3–5-inch), 30–40 water snails (such as great pond or ramshorn), and 15 bunches of submerged plants.

■ **Know your water:** Invest in a kit for water testing. They're inexpensive and several types are available. Test for ammonia and nitrite levels when you first fill your pond and then periodically thereafter, particularly if your fish are dying. If you do have a chemical problem, treating the pond with bacteria that remove excess nitrogen or a partial water change, described below, can help lower ammonia and nitrite levels.

■ **Keep it filled:** Don't let the pond water level drop more than an inch or so. When the pond's normal water level drops, the liner is exposed to deteriorating UV rays.

Most city tap water contains chloramine, a chemical compound that is dangerous to fish. If the amount of water added to the pond at any time is less than 20 percent of the total water volume of the pond, the natural nitrogen in the pond will break down the ammonia bond in the chloramine structure, and all will be fine. However, if you need to add more than 20 percent tap water, then also add the correct amount of chloramine remover as indicated on the container instructions.

When you add tap water to your pond, fill the pond slowly in an area away from the fish so they can't play in it. Ideal spots include in the filter or waterfall area. Another alternative is to put a sock over the hose end and place it at the bottom of the pond. Let the water run slowly through the sock so if you forget to turn off the water, there is not a rapid change in the new water volume.

You can avoid all the hassle and risk of topping up a pond by hand by installing an auto float valve (see page 29). It is a device mounted in the pond that automatically refills it to the predetermined set line whenever the water level drops.

■ **Provide aeration:** In a healthy, ecologically balanced pond, extra aeration should not be necessary. However, the additional aeration provided by a fountain or waterfall can provide the extra oxygen necessary to support fish that are overstocked in a pond. Bear in mind that the fish load in any healthy pond is increasing daily as the fish grow and multiply. In addition, during the peak of summer heat, water holds less oxygen than at cooler temperatures. You may find it necessary to provide aeration for your pond by midsummer even if it is not needed at the beginning of the year.

If you don't have a fountain, or if it's not strong enough to aerate the water and the fish are gulping for air at the surface, add a pump with an air stone at the bottom of the pond, lower the nitrogen level in the pond, or thin out your fish population.

■ **Keep the pond free of leaves and debris:** Pinch off yellowing and dying leaves; they can turn into pollutants if left unattended. If tree leaves are a problem in autumn, put a net over the pool to catch them or make skimming the pond a daily routine.

In late fall, when you remove the pump for the winter, make sure the water is free of debris before the pond ices over.

■ **Keep it under control:** If fish numbers get out of hand, give some away. Thin out invasive plants regularly and divide overgrown plants so that no one element begins to take over.

■ **Consider a filter:** If the garden pool has continuing problems with debris, too much sunlight, or excessive fish waste, consider adding a biological filter to the pool setup. See page 30 for more information on filters.

■ **Prevent run-off:** When fertilizing or applying other chemicals around your garden pool, make sure that the materials don't get into the water. Some are toxic to fish, and others can promote algae growth in the water.

■ **Feed fish properly:** Feed fish only what they can devour in about a minute. Don't feed them unless they are ravenous.

In hot weather, don't worry if the fish don't seem to be eating much. In summer, they'll feed on insects and plants. Feeding fish too much or too often will foul the water and throw off its balance of nitrogen and oxygen.

CONTROLLING ALGAE

One of the most common signs of imbalance in a water garden is free-floating algae, which makes the water green and murky. In severe cases, algae can coat and choke out other plants. It can also stress the fish.

Certain kinds of algae are good for ponds, however. Smooth algae, for example, grows on the liner and on pots. It is a sign of a healthy pond and gives a water garden an attractive patina, making it look as though it has been there a while. In fact, smooth algae growth is called a passive filter because it removes nutrients that feed other, less desirable, algae.

Filamentous and tufted algae (sometimes called blanketweed or string algae), as well as floating phytoplankton algae, are not desirable. These grow in long, ropey, dark green colonies.

All garden ponds, especially during the first two to three weeks after they're constructed or cleaned, have excess algae. Most will have an algae bloom each spring, too, as the pond struggles to reestablish its balance. But as your floating plants grow and begin to shade the water and compete with the algae for light, the water should clear.

Fish are useful in your fight against algae because they eat some of the invasive varieties. Pond snails, which you can buy from a water garden supplier or through the mail, also are voracious algae eaters.

Algae grows rapidly in warm, stagnant water, so keep your pond filled, especially in hot weather. Deep ponds warm up more slowly than shallow pools.

Filamentous algae, which looks like floating seaweed, should be removed from the surface of the water by hand or with a rake. If it forms on rocks or waterfalls, turn off the pump and let the algae dry. Then you can scrape and brush it off. If that doesn't work, rewet the algae and sprinkle it with non-iodized table salt, such as pickling and canning salt. Leave for several hours then brush off. Salt, as long as it is used only rarely and in moderation, kills the algae, but doesn't harm fish.

Use algicides with caution. They may stunt plant growth necessary for a good garden-pool balance. If algae occurs on a regular basis, a biological filter (see page 30) may be in order for your pool. Consider adding a UV clarifier (see page 31), which not only defends your pond from suspended algae, but also destroys many bacteria, viruses, and fungi that could harm fish.

SEASONAL MAINTENANCE

Even the most ecologically balanced pond will need regular maintenance to keep it and the plants healthy. Of course, ponds in different parts of the country will require different care. In southern California and Florida, there is no concern about ponds freezing over in winter. In dry regions, ponds do not benefit from the reionization, or introduction of fresh rainwater, and natural cleansing provided by rain and lightning. Thus, hose water has to be added more frequently.

Spring

■ **Perform systems check and spring cleaning:** Check your equipment such as pumps, filters, and electrical sources to make sure everything is in good working order. Test the ground-fault circuit interrupters (GFCIs). Use a net to clean out bottom waste from the pond, or vacuum the bottom with a hose-operated pond sweep for ponds up to 12 feet in diameter or a wet/dry vacuum for very small ponds.

Begin running filters and pumps. If your pond was shut down for the winter, once the water begins to warm, it's time to turn the filters and pumps back on.

■ **Divide and feed plants:** See pages 84 to 85 for instructions on how to maintain plants. Use the same techniques for dividing any clump-forming marginal plant that you would for dividing hardy water lilies.

Plant and begin fertilizing. Introduce any new aquatic plants to your pond, and start a monthly plant-feeding program with fertilizer pellets formulated for underwater plants. Once water temperatures reach 60°F–70°F, place tropical water lilies in the pond, or replant overwintered bulbs.

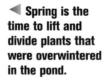

◀ **Spring is the time to lift and divide plants that were overwintered in the pond.**

▶ **In the summer, keep the water level topped off. It's better to add a small amount daily than a large amount of water once a week.**

Summer

■ **Keep the pond clean:** Use a net to skim off any leaves or debris floating on the water surface. Empty the skimmer basket. Remove dead or dying leaves from plants in or around the pond on a weekly basis, and deadhead spent flowers. Scoop off filamentous algae if it becomes a problem, and use it to mulch garden beds.

■ **Top off water level:** If the pond level drops, add water. It's all right to use the chlorinated water from the garden hose as long as you add no more than 5–10 percent of the total pond volume at a time. It's better to add small quantities daily than to top up with a large amount once a week.

■ **Clean filters:** If you have mechanical filters and/or skimmers, they should be cleaned on a weekly or even twice-weekly schedule. Hose off and dry the filter pad before replacing it so excess bacteria don't build up. Ideally you should have a spare pad so one can dry while the other is in use. If you wait longer, the nitrosoma bacteria will form a hard encrustation, similar to lava rock, that will destroy the filter's effectiveness.

■ **Periodically check water quality:** Water-quality test kits to measure ammonia, pH, chlorine, and chloramine levels are most accurate when the water temperature is 80°F, or warmer. Ideal garden pool water pH is between 7.5 and 10.5. Check these levels in the morning, between 8 and 10 a.m.

■ **Check fish for diseases:** Be on the lookout for these indications of unhealthy fish: sluggishness, clamped fins, hovering in a corner, abnormal blotching, and ragged fins or tails. Consult a professional if you detect a problem.

◀ **In the summer and fall, gently net the fish so you can closely examine them for signs of disease or stress.**

Autumn

■ **Clean bottom of pond:** As in the spring, use a net to scoop out bottom debris, or vacuum the bottom.

■ **Stop fertilizing:** About six weeks before the first frost, stop fertilizing the plants.

■ **Remove fallen leaves:** Be vigilant about removing fallen leaves from the pond surface. Some people find it helpful to cover the pond with a fine-mesh net to make leaf removal easier.

■ **Provide hiding places for fish:** Provide shelter, such as sections of 4-inch drainpipe, for fish to use as safe holes from predators when the foliage has died back.

Winter

In warm-winter climates, continue your routine maintenance. No special winter care is required. In cold-weather climates, the overwintering measures depend on the severity of your local weather.

■ **Lower depth of hardy plants:** Lower the plants so they are deep enough to keep the roots from freezing, normally at least 36 inches in cold climates. You also can overwinter tender hardy marginals in deep, ice-free water. The less cold-sensitive marginals can stay in place.

■ **Stop feeding fish:** Koi can survive over winter as long as they have a deep (usually 2-foot) area in the pond that won't freeze. Once water temperatures drop below 50°F, they go into a state of semi-hibernation in this area below the water freeze line. They need no supplemental food in this state.

▶ **Garden pools are as spectacular in the winter as they are the rest of the year. Winter pond maintenance primarily involves keeping the water from freezing solid so the fish can breathe.**

■ **Open hole in ice sheet:** If ice completely covers the pond, the fish will die from trapped gases, so you need to maintain a breathing hole in the ice. Keep an electric pond deicer running all winter. Do not hammer a hole in the ice. The shock waves will injure or kill the fish. In mild-winter areas (no lower than –10°F), an air pump with an air stone should be enough to prevent freezing, particularly for ponds of 1,000 gallons or more. In milder climates, a piece of floating plastic foam 1 foot square and 2 inches thick will keep ice from forming. Also remove heavy snow cover from the pond surface. Darkness leads to algae die off, causing oxygen depletion.

Another option is to build a frame to support a pond cover made from plastic sheeting. Cover the pond nightly no matter how mild the temperatures are predicted to be, and use a pond deicer to keep the water temperature even. Uncover during the day to allow air to circulate.

■ **Care in extreme climates:** Pools made of porous materials such as concrete, brick, masonry, or tile can crack in freeze-thaw cycles, as will some ponds made from a rigid liner. Drain the pool, and drain or remove any plumbing. Also drain wall and freestanding fountains. Store hardy plants in their pots, double bagged and sealed in a dark location that remains between 50°F and 60°F. Keep the soil damp. Keep fish in as large a container as practical; galvanized metal is not suitable. Filter and aerate the water, and cover the container with a screen so the fish cannot jump out.

GALLERY OF PLANTS

▼ Water gardens can contain a wonderful variety of unusual plants. In addition to being attractive, water plants are integral to the pond's health. And, an abundance of wildlife depend on plants for food and shelter.

Plants are the crowning jewels of water gardens. They add beauty with color, texture, and scent. There is an incredible variety of water plants from which to choose for your garden pool—hardy plants, tropical plants, fragrant plants, plants that flower, plants grown for foliage, huge plants and tiny plants, plants for the sun and plants for the shade.

Water garden plants are diverse in their growing habitats as well. Bog plants grow where the water table is high, but the plants are not constantly in standing water. Marginal plants are sun-loving plants that thrive in standing water. (Many marginals also grow well in drier sites.) They are usually planted at the edge, or margin, of a pond. Floating plant roots protrude into the water and need no soil at all, though they may take root in shallow water. Their tops float on the surface. Submerged plants grow completely underwater. They keep the water clear by absorbing nutrients and carbon dioxide, and thus starve out algae. In addition they add oxygen to the water. Deep-water plants include water lilies and lotuses. Their large leaves shade the water surface and keep it cool, while the roots provide food and shelter for fish.

The value of water garden plants is much deeper than appearance. In addition to lovely flowers, foliage, or fragrance, aquatic plants keep the water clear and healthy. They also provide food and shelter for all kinds of wildlife, including fish, waterfowl, amphibians, beneficial insects, butterflies, and birds. You can have a water feature without plants, but maintaining a healthy ecological balance is much easier when you include an assortment of plants in your plans. Not only will you make pond maintenance easier by including plants, you'll be able to enjoy cyclical changes in your water garden highlighted by the seasonal variations in plant features.

PLANT GALLERY

Aruncus dioicus, syn. *A. sylvester*
Goatsbeard

- **Hardiness zones: 3–7**
- **Heat zones: 7–1**
- **Light: Part sun or full shade**
- **Size: 4–6'H × 5'W**
- **Features: Creamy white flowers**

Goatsbeard, *A. dioicus*

Fine, feathery foliage and 8-inch-long panicles of fluffy white flowers adorn this moisture-loving plant.
Siting: Plant goatsbeard 2½ feet apart in moist to wet, fertile soil. It will grow in soil with a pH that is mildly acidic (6.1) to mildly alkaline (7.8). It prefers morning sun and afternoon shade, but tolerates full shade.
Foliage and flowers: Feathery, fernlike leaves grow 3 feet long. Creamy white inflorescences adorn goatsbeard in early and midsummer.
Care: Goatsbeard needs summer days with high heat to perform best. Cut stems down to an inch above the ground in autumn.
Propagation: Direct-sow seeds outdoors in autumn or divide plants in early spring or autumn. Allow the seed heads to dry on the plants. The plants also will self-sow.
Noteworthy plants: 'Kneiffii' is smaller than the species, growing 3 feet tall.

Astilbe spp.
Astilbe

- **Hardiness zones: 3–9**
- **Heat zones: 8–1**
- **Light: Full sun to half shade**
- **Size: 20–48" H × 24" W**
- **Features: Feathery flowers in pink, red, or white**

With handsome, toothed foliage and feathery pink, red, or white flowers, astilbe is a superb addition to a bog garden.
Siting: Astilbe is adaptable to varied soil types, but prefers fertile, moist, well-drained, and acidic soil. The drier the soil, the more shade astilbe requires.
Foliage and flowers: Flower panicles bloom in early to late summer, depending on the species and hybrid.
Care: Astilbes are heavy feeders. Fertilize them in the spring before growth starts, and again, lightly, in the fall after the first frost. Divide them every 3 to 4 years. If powdery mildew strikes, clean up any leaf debris around the plant, and control with a fungicide. Follow label directions, and make sure spray does not drift into nearby water.
Propagation: Divide large clumps in autumn or early spring.
Noteworthy plants: 'Deutchland' flowers pure white in late spring (20 inches tall); 'Sprite' boasts shell pink flowers in summer (20 inches tall); and 'Fanal' has crimson flowers in early summer (24 inches tall).

Astilbe, *A.* 'Visions'

Eupatorium purpureum
Joe-Pye weed

- **Hardiness zones: 3–9**
- **Heat zones: 9–1**
- **Light: Sun or part shade**
- **Size: 7'H × 3'W**
- **Features: Purple leaves; pink flowers**

Joe-Pye weed, *E. purpureum*

A stately, clump-forming perennial that thrives in alkaline soil, Joe-Pye weed is a towering giant of a plant that develops purple-tinged leaves and pink flowers. Another common name is purple boneset, because the stems are purple at the joints.
Siting: Plant Joe-Pye weed 1½ feet apart in sun or part shade in moist, alkaline soil.
Foliage and flowers: Ten-inch-long whorls of lance-shape leaves grow on upright purplish stems. Domed clusters of fragrant pale pink to pale purple flowers adorn the stately plants from midsummer to early autumn.
Care: Watch for snails and slugs. If powdery mildew, rust, or white smut appear, treat them with fungicide.
Propagation: Divide clumps in early spring.
Noteworthy plants: *E. maculatum* (USDA Zones 5–11) produces lightly scented, pale purple flowers up to 8 inches across in late July to early September. It is very showy when grown in mass plantings.

Hemerocallis hybrids
Daylily

- **Hardiness zones: 3–10**
- **Heat zones: 12–2**
- **Light: Sun or light shade**
- **Size: 30–48"H × 30–48"W**
- **Features: Red, yellow, orange, or pink flowers; grassy foliage**

Daylilies are easy-to-grow, clump-forming perennials that thrive in moist soil. By combining different cultivars (there are 30,000 to choose from!), you can have flowers all summer long.

Siting: Grow daylilies in sun or light shade; they are excellent in drifts along a pond edge. Excessive shade will reduce flowering. Daylilies do best with a soil pH between 6.5 and 7 (slightly acid to neutral).

Foliage and flowers: Modern hybrids are available in a wide spectrum of colors from palest yellow to vibrant red, pink, lavender, royal purple, white, and even black. Flower forms include circular, stellate, spider-shape, triangular, single, and double. Some are scented. Each bloom lasts only one day (or one night in the case of nocturnal varieties that open in late afternoon), but a succession of flowers keeps interest high for several weeks. With the right mix, you can have flowers starting in early summer and continuing through autumn.

Care: Mulch plants in late

Daylilies and ferns combine here.

autumn. Fertilize with a balanced liquid fertilizer every 2–3 weeks in the spring. Divide when the flower production wanes and flower size shrinks, approximately every 3–5 years. Snails enjoy tender shoots.

Propagation: Divide hardy daylilies in spring or autumn; evergreen species and cultivars in spring.

Daylilies grow well at water's edge.

Noteworthy plants: 'Glacier Bay', with 5½-inch creamy white flowers with gold ruffle and green throat, blooms in mid-season, and reblooms. 'Magic Obsession' sports 5-inch purple flowers with a gold ruffle and green throat early to mid-season, and reblooms. 'Dan Tau' has 6-inch cream-green with pink suffusion and lime-green halo blooms early in season, and reblooms. 'Alec Allen' has flowers that are 5½-inch creamy yellow with lime-green throat, which bloom early to mid-season, and reblooms. 'Always Afternoon' features 5½-inch medium mauve flowers edged buff with a purple eye zone and a green throat that open early in the season, and reblooms. 'Annie Go Lightly' has 7-inch bright red blossoms with greenish throats, which open in mid- to late season. 'Barbara Mitchell' features 6-inch pink blossoms with a green throat in mid-season, and reblooms. *H. fulva* and *H. lilio-asphodelus* are aggressive spreaders unsuitable for small gardens.

Hosta spp.
Hosta

- **Hardiness zones: 3–9**
- **Heat zones: 9–2**
- **Light: Part shade in South; morning sun in North**
- **Size: 3–30"H × 3–48"W**
- **Features: Wide range of foliage colors and textures as well as variegations; flowers on tall, bare stems in summer.**

Hostas are unusual because they flourish in very wet situations, but also tolerate drought. There are about 70 species of hosta, and thousands of hybrids.

Siting: Grow in moist, fertile soil.

Foliage and flowers: Grown more for their foliage than flowers, hosta leaves vary from shades of green, blue, or yellow; some leaves are edged with cream, gold, or white variegations. The leaf texture may be crinkled, smooth, shiny, or deeply veined. Tubular white or lavender-blue blossoms open in summer.

Care: Wrap roots in chicken wire to protect from moles. Snails, slugs, and deer eat the foliage.

Propagation: Sow seeds in spring, or divide clumps in late summer or early spring.

Noteworthy plants: *H. plantaginea* and *H.* 'Fragrant Bouquet' are deliciously fragrant. 'Royal Standard' has crinkly green leaves, and 'Touch of Class' has heart-shaped leaves with blue edges and yellow centers.

Hosta, *H.* 'Sultana'

Iris ensata
Japanese iris

- **Hardiness zones: 3–9**
- **Heat zones: 9–1**
- **Light: Full sun, part shade in the South**
- **Size: 3'H × 3'W**
- **Features: Purple, pink, white or blue flowers**

Japanese iris, *I. ensata*

Japanese iris are easy to grow; they bloom in June and July.
Siting: Grow Japanese iris in full sun (part shade in the South) in rich, acid soil. They prefer constant moisture during the growing season and well-drained soil in winter. Most iris are unsuitable for the dry heat of the desert Southwest.
Foliage and flowers: Lance-shaped leaves remain all season. Blue, purple, and white, butterfly-like flowers open in midsummer.
Care: Greedy feeders, give them rich, acid soil; fertilize after flowering and when new leaves appear. Divide and repot with fresh soil every three years in fall. Remove pots from the water in fall and bury them in well-drained garden soil until spring. Give extra winter protection in USDA Zone 4 or colder.
Propagation: Divide in autumn.
Noteworthy plants: 'Mt. Fuji' is pure white with three yellow spots, called signals. Also consider *I. sibirica*, Siberian iris, which blooms in a variety of hybridized colors.

Ligularia dentata
Bigleaf ligularia, golden groundsel

- **Hardiness zones: 4–8**
- **Heat zones: 8–1**
- **Light: Part sun with midday shade**
- **Size: 3–5'H × 3'W**
- **Features: Large, leathery, heart-shaped leaves and sprays of daisylike yellow flowers.**

Bold foliage and sunny yellow flowers from midsummer to autumn make bigleaf ligularia a great accent plant.
Siting: Plant 1½ feet apart in reliably moist soil in part sun protected from strong winds. Soil should be moist to wet.
Foliage and flowers: Round or kidney-shaped leaves are 12 inches across. From summer to autumn, it produces clusters of daisylike yellow flowers.
Care: Protect emergent shoots from snails and slugs.
Propagation: Surface-sow seed in pots of compost kept slightly moist. Germination usually takes one to six months. Divide plants in spring.
Noteworthy plants: 'Desdemona' has yellow-orange flowers and brownish-green leaves with maroon underneath; 'Othello' has large purple, bronze, or green leaves with maroon undersides and stems.

Bigleaf ligularia, *L. dentata* 'Desdemona'

Mimulus × hybridus
Monkey flower

- **Hardiness zones: 6–9**
- **Heat zones: 10–1**
- **Light: Part shade**
- **Size: 8"H × 12"W**
- **Features: Bushy, branching plant with oval, toothed leaves and tubular, spotted flowers**

Monkey flower, *M.* 'Andean Nymph'

Discovered in Chile in the early 1970s, the monkey flower is a beautiful, moisture-loving plant that thrives in half sun, half shade. It enlivens the garden with tubular scarlet, orange, or yellow flowers, some with speckles.
Siting: Plant monkey flower 8 inches apart in part to full shade in moist, humus-rich, fertile soil with a neutral pH. It needs summer days with high heat, although it does not like high humidity.
Foliage and flowers: Monkey flower is an erect, branching plant with elliptical leaves and tubular, brightly colored flowers, usually spotted, in summer.
Care: After flowering, trim plants lightly to encourage a second flush of blooms.
Propagation: Divide in spring or take softwood cuttings in early summer.
Noteworthy plants: 'Calypso' is a mixture of single-colored, bicolored, and spotted flowers in a wide range of colors.

Primula japonica
Japanese primrose

- **Hardiness zones: 4–8**
- **Heat zones: 8–1**
- **Light: Part shade; full sun if kept moist**
- **Size: 18"W × 18"H**
- **Features: Clusters of white, red, pink, and yellow flowers**

By growing different species, you can have primroses in flower from late winter through midsummer. Although considered the queen of bog garden plants, they languish in the hot southern summers in heat zone 8 or warmer, which includes most of the southern United States.

Siting: Plant in part shade in rich, moist, neutral to acidic loam. Will tolerate sun if kept very moist. Space plants half the distance of their mature width.

Foliage and flowers: In early to midsummer, stems bearing whorls of flowers 1 inch across in shades ranging from pure white to deep red grow out of light green rosettes of finely scalloped or serrated, oblong-shaped foliage.

Care: Mulch in spring, divide every two to three years in spring or autumn, and deadhead blooms that are finished.

Candelabra primrose, *P. bulleyana*

Japanese primrose, *P. japonica*

Propagation: Divide primroses in early spring. Primroses self-seed freely and overtime will make a large colony.

Noteworthy plants: For a constant succession of bloom, start with *Primula rosea* which flowers earliest in the season with rose

Primrose, *P. rosea*

pink blossoms. A month later, *P. denticulata* produces lavender, white, blue, or pale purple flowers with small yellow eyes on 3-inch-wide spherical heads. Next in succession are the Candelabra primroses which flower in whorls spaced along the stem. *P. japonica* is one type of candelabra primrose. Hybrids include 'Inverewe' with scarlet

flowers, 'Miller's Crimson' with deep crimson blossoms, and 'Postford White' which is a pure and brilliant white. Tall-growing *P. pulverulenta* (tubular red flowers with dark eyes), *P. chungensis* (pale orange flowers), *P. burmanica* (yellow-eyed, rosy-purple or pink blooms), and *P. bulleyana*

Primrose, *P. denticulata*

(yellow-orange flowers) are also candelabra primroses. A little later in the season, *P. sikkimensis* opens its umbels of fragrant white, yellow, or cream flowers. Last to go on display is *P. florindae* which produces fragrant bright yellow blossoms.

Primrose, *P. florindae*

Rheum palmatum
Chinese rhubarb

- **Hardiness zones: 5–9**
- **Heat zones: 9–1**
- **Light: Full sun or part shade**
- **Size: 6–8'H × 6'W**
- **Features: Large, dramatic specimen plant with cream to red flower panicles**

Chinese rhubarb, *R. palmatum tanguticum*

Its tall stature and large jagged leaves that have a reddish hue when young make Chinese rhubarb an outstanding focal point in a bog garden.

Siting: Grow Chinese rhubarb in humus-rich, moist soil in full sun or part shade.

Foliage and flowers: Thick leaf stalks support 36-inch-wide dark green leaves that are purple-red and hairy underneath. In late spring and early summer, plumes of pink, red, or white starry flowers stand tall above bold toothed foliage.

Care: Mulch annually in spring with well-rotted manure or compost. Chinese rhubarb is susceptible to root and crown rot, rust, and Southern blight. Avoid heavy clay soil, and start with healthy plants.

Propagation: Sow seeds in fall, or divide crowns in early spring.

Noteworthy plants: 'Ace of Hearts' is a dwarf variety that grows 4 feet tall. *R.* 'Atrosanguineum' and *R.* 'Bowles Crimson' have purplish foliage and bear crimson flowers.

Rodgersia pinnata
Featherleaf rodgersia

- **Hardiness zones: 3–7**
- **Heat zones: 7–1**
- **Light: Full sun or part shade**
- **Size: 48"H × 30"W**
- **Features: Dramatic specimen**

A native of China, featherleaf rodgersia is a worthy import. The 36-inch-long, palmate leaves are reason enough to grow this plant. Showy flower plumes standing tall above the foliage in mid- and late summer add to the plant's allure.

Siting: Plant rodgersia in sun or part shade in moist, humus-rich soil. It will tolerate some drought in deeper shade.

Foliage and flowers: The emerald green, often bronzed or red-tinged leaves are deeply veined with a crinkly texture. They stand tall on reddish-green stalks. Starry pink or white tiny flowers blossom on tall, fluffy panicles in mid- to late summer.

Care: Rodgersia has no serious insect or disease problems, although snails and slugs are attracted to its foliage.

Propagation: Divide clumps in early spring.

Noteworthy plants: Young leaves on 'Superba' are purplish bronze, and the flowers are bright pink. 'Alba' grows just 3 feet tall, and is hardy only to Zone 5. It has small starry white flowers on fluffy panicles.

Featherleaf rodgersia, *R. pinnata* 'Superba'

Trollius ×cultorum
Globeflower

- **Hardiness zones: 5–8**
- **Heat zones: 8–5**
- **Light: Full sun or part shade**
- **Size: 36"H × 18"W**
- **Features: Sunny yellow flowers**

Globeflower, *T. ×cultorum*

Globeflower's large, cup-shape yellow flowers add a splash of sunshine to bog gardens. Choose from a selection of cultivars to get the plant height and the intensity of flower color you want.

Siting: Globeflower flourishes in moist, fertile, deep soil in full sun or partial shade.

Foliage and flowers: Glossy, lance-shape leaves that have five lobes and are toothed cluster around the plant base with smaller stem leaves. Globular, buttercup-like flowers ranging in color from pale primrose-yellow to bold orange-yellow, depending on hybrid, bloom from mid-spring to midsummer.

Care: Mulch in spring and divide clumps every three years.

Propagation: Sow seed when it is ripe, or divide as new growth appears or just after flowering.

Noteworthy plants: 'Alabaster' has primrose yellow flowers and grows 24 inches tall; 'Feuertroll' has rich orange-yellow flowers; 'Orange Globe' is taller at 30 inches and produces bright orange flowers.

Acorus calamus
Sweet flag

- ■ **Hardiness zones: 4–11**
- ■ **Heat zones: 12–2**
- ■ **Light: Full sun or part shade**
- ■ **Size: 30"H×24"W**
- ■ **Features: Iris-like foliage**

Sweet flag is an iris-like plant with long pointed leaves that emit a citrus fragrance when crushed. It will not overrun an earth-bottom pond.

Siting: Grow in full sun to light shade in soil with a neutral pH. Set plants 5–6 inches under the water surface, and no deeper than 9 inches.

Foliage and flowers: Sweet flag is primarily grown for its foliage.

Care: Sweet flag is free of pests and diseases. Divide when clumps grow too large or dense, approximately every 3–4 years.

Propagation: Divide rhizomes in autumn or early spring and replant them in shallow water.

Noteworthy plants: 'Variegatus' with striped leaves is considered one of the finest ornamentals for wet situations.

Sweet flag, *A. calamus* 'Variegatus'

Asclepias incarnata
Swamp milkweed

- ■ **Hardiness zones: 3–9**
- ■ **Heat zones: 9–2**
- ■ **Light: Full sun**
- ■ **Size: 48"H×24"W**
- ■ **Features: Flower umbels attract butterflies**

Swamp milkweed, *A. incarnata*

Swamp milkweed grows wild at the edge of swamps and ponds. Because of its weedy nature, it is best suited to naturalistic ponds.

Siting: Grow swamp milkweed in full sun in moist, sandy soil with a neutral pH.

Foliage and flowers: Elliptic mid-green leaves grow on thick-stemmed branches. Pink-purple, fragrant flowers blossom from summer into autumn, followed by silky seed heads.

Care: Protect from slugs, especially young spring growth.

Propagation: Divide swamp milkweed in spring, taking care since this plant suffers setback with root disturbance. Or, you can take cuttings in late spring. Cut 4-inch-long shoots with as much of the white underground stem as possible. Plant in pots and keep in a shaded, moist spot until rooted.

Noteworthy plants: 'Ice Ballet' is a long-blooming bright white selection with mildly fragrant flowers. 'Soulmate' typically grows 3–3½ feet tall with mildly fragrant deep rose-pink flowers.

Caltha palustris
Marsh marigold

- ■ **Hardiness zones: 3–7**
- ■ **Heat zones: 7–1**
- ■ **Light: Full sun or part shade**
- ■ **Size: 12–18"H×10"W**
- ■ **Features: Buttercup yellow flowers**

Marsh marigold flowers early in the season for a month or more. It goes dormant in midsummer, so grow it near other plants to fill the void.

Siting: Grow marsh marigold in groups in full sun or part shade, spaced 12–18 inches apart in moist soil or water no deeper than 1–6 inches.

Foliage and flowers: Kidney-shape dark-green leaves grow up to 4 inches long. Waxy yellow flowers open in spring and early summer.

Care: To avoid fungal problems, be sure to select healthy, disease-free plants, and space them so they have good air circulation. Avoid handling the plants when the foliage is wet.

Propagation: Divide root clumps before flowers appear in early spring or when plants are dormant in summer. Sow seed in early summer as soon as it is ripe. Seed-grown plants tend not to bloom until the second year.

Noteworthy plants: 'Plena' has yellow double blossoms; 'Alba' flowers white.

Marsh marigold, *C. palustris*

Canna flaccida, C. glauca
Water canna

- **Hardiness zones: 8–11**
- **Heat zones: 12–1**
- **Light: Full sun**
- **Size: 2–10'H × 2'W**
- **Features: Tropical foliage, vivid flowers**

Water canna, *C. glauca*

Water canna, *C. flaccida*

Water canna, *C. 'Australia'*

Water cannas and their hybrids and terrestrial cannas that tolerate water are an excellent addition to a pondside garden. True water cannas, including those called Longwood hybrids, grow well in saturated soil with water over their crowns. Water-tolerant cannas have adapted to wet conditions but grow well in average soil as well. Experiment with your favorite terrestrial canna to discover if it will grow in water.

Siting: Grow in full sun near or in the water up to a depth of 6 inches. Space 9–12 inches apart. Water cannas like baking heat and plenty of moisture.

Foliage and flowers: Large, broad foliage resembling banana leaves give water cannas a tropical look. In many cultivars, the foliage is striped with yellow, orange, or red. From early summer through the fall, cannas flower in a wide variety of colors ranging from pink and yellow, to shades of red and orange. Hummingbirds love to sip nectar from the flowers.

Care: Fertilize cannas monthly.

Remove spent flowers and leaves, and cut off the top portion of the flower stalk once all the blossoms are finished to encourage more blooms. To renew, cut the plant to the ground, fertilize (manure is ideal), and give plenty of water. Where winter temperatures remain above 0°F, leave them in the ground. In colder climates, lift and clean the tubers and store in a ventilated container with barely moist sand or peat moss in a frost-free area. Replant in spring when water temperature is hovering at 65°F. Alternatively, overwinter a plant indoors in a warm, sunny spot. It will grow leggy, but will return to a healthy appearance once set outdoors in spring. Remove aphids with a strong spray of water or, for heavy

Water canna, *C. glauca* 'Erebus'

infestations, with insecticidal soap (remove plant from pond before treating). Handpick Japanese beetles and throw them in the water to feed the fish (the beetles can't swim). If spider mites or mealy bugs are a problem on an overwintered live plant, remove contaminated stalks at the base of the plant and discard. Large orange spots on the leaves indicate canna rust. Good sanitation is the best prevention. If rust develops, cut all the stalks back to the soil line and discard leaves.

Propagation: Divide rhizomes in spring, making sure each has a prominent "eye." Before sowing seeds in spring or autumn, nick them or soak in warm water for 24 hours. Seeds don't grow true to type.

Noteworthy plants: 'Australia' has deep maroon-black, satiny foliage, shocking red flowers, and grows 4–5 feet tall. 'African Sunset' grows 7 feet tall, and has burgundy-purple foliage striped yellow and red, with melon-orange flowers. 'Red Futurity' is a dwarf canna (2–3 feet tall) with broad dark burgundy foliage and deep red blooms. It does well in containers in or near the pond. 'Florence Vaughn' grows 6 feet tall and produces large bright yellow flowers highlighted with dramatic orange-red speckling.

Colocasia esculenta
Taro, elephant's ear

- Hardiness zones: 9–11
- Heat zones: 12–10
- Light: Full sun to part shade
- Size: 2–6'H×2–4'W
- Features: Large, dramatic foliage

The primary ingredient of poi, taro is grown in gardens for its large arrow- or heart-shaped leaves, and is a showy plant for use around water features.
Siting: Plant in fertile, organically rich, medium-wet to wet soils (submerged up to 6 inches) in full sun or part shade. The leaves grow bigger in part shade.
Foliage and flowers: Grown for foliage interest, taro has large, veined leaves shaped like an elephant's ear. The flower, which is not particularly showy, is a spathe that grows to 15 inches long.
Care: Fertilize taro regularly. In cold climates, overwinter indoors in pots, or dig and store corms in vermiculite in a cool, dark spot. Yearly transplanting helps keep plants vigorous.
Propagation: Divide corms from the main plant or take divisions from "hulis," which sprout from the top or side.
Noteworthy plants: 'Black Magic' has purple-black leaves; 'Metallica' has deep purple stems and blue-green leaves.

Taro, *C. esculenta* 'Black Magic'

Cyperus alternifolius
Umbrella palm

- Hardiness zones: 8–11
- Heat zones: 12–6
- Light: Full sun to part shade
- Size: 2–3'H×2–3'W
- Features: Decorative foliage

Umbrella palm, *C. alternifolius*

A perennial sedge naturalized in rivers of northern Africa, umbrella palm is a cousin of papyrus, which was used by the Egyptians to make paper.
Siting: Grow this plant in sun or part shade in boggy soil or standing water up to 12 inches deep. In small ponds, grow it in containers to keep it from spreading invasively.
Foliage and flowers: Umbrella palm is grown for its feathery clusters of rays on top of tall stalks. Tiny brown flowers bloom at the end of each ray.
Care: Umbrella palm is a low-maintenance plant. When stems inside old clumps die, dig up the plant, divide, and discard the dead portion. In hardiness Zone 8, freezing temperatures will kill the top, but the plant will recover if the roots are mulched or are under water.
Propagation: Divide in the spring.
Noteworthy plants: 'Nana' is a dwarf variety that grows 2–3 feet tall and spreads to 18–24 inches.

Equisetum hyemale
Horsetail

- Hardiness zones: 3–11
- Heat zones: 12–1
- Light: Full sun to partial shade
- Size: 4'H×indefinite spread
- Features: Green, jointed stems with black highlights

Often grown in Japanese-style gardens, at the edge of ponds, and in the margins of ornamental water gardens, horsetail has upright, bamboo-like dark green stems.
Siting: Plant in full sun or part shade in medium-wet to wet soils or in up to 4 inches of standing water. Declared a weed in many countries, horsetail is extremely invasive and difficult to remove because rhizomes spread wide and deep. Any portion of remaining rhizome can sprout a new plant. Grow in containers sunk in the ground with the lip just above ground level to contain the spread.
Foliage and flowers: Horsetail is grown for the evergreen stems that resemble bamboo.
Care: There are no serious insect or disease problems.
Propagation: Divide horsetail in spring or autumn.
Noteworthy plants: *E. scirpoides* is a smaller, much less invasive version of horsetail than *E. hyemale*. It grows 8 inches tall and spreads indefinitely.

Dwarf horsetail, *E. scirpoides*

Iris laevigata
Japanese water iris

- ■ **Hardiness zones: 3–9**
- ■ **Heat zones: 9–1**
- ■ **Light: Sun or part shade**
- ■ **Size: 16"H×indefinite spread**
- ■ **Features: Upright, lancelike foliage and a bold flower display in summer**

Plant a selection of water iris species for a variety of flower forms and colors. They are all useful to provide vertical interest in both formal and informal water garden settings.

Japanese water iris, *I. laevigata* 'Variegata'

Siting: Plant in sun to part shade in damp soil or shallow water spaced 14 inches apart.
Foliage and flowers: Purple-blue flowers with standards much shorter than their falls open in early and midsummer. Clumps of upright, long, narrow leaves add vertical interest in season.
Care: Greedy feeders, give iris rich, acid soil. Fertilize after flowering and when new leaves

Louisiana iris, *I.* 'Inner Beauty'

Yellow flag, *I. pseudacorus*

appear in spring. Divide and repot with fresh soil every three years in fall. They can remain in water all year.
Propagation: Divide rhizomes in late summer or early autumn.
Noteworthy plants: 'Variegata' has pale lavender flowers and green-and-white-striped foliage that provides a much longer season of interest than the regular all-green variety, and looks good with a wide range of pondside

Blue flag, *I. versicolor*

and bog garden plants. For a longer display of iris in and near your pond, also plant yellow flag (*I. pseudacorus*), which has yellow flowers in spring, and blue flag (*I. versicolor*) for its blue flowers with yellow and white markings that open in late spring and early summer.

Lobelia cardinalis
Cardinal flower

- ■ **Hardiness zones: 2–8**
- ■ **Heat zones: 8–1**
- ■ **Light: Full sun to part shade**
- ■ **Size: 12–36"H×12"W**
- ■ **Features: Bright red flower spikes**

Cardinal flower, *L. cardinalis*

Highly attractive to butterflies and hummingbirds, cardinal flower makes a red exclamation mark along a pond margin.
Siting: Plant cardinal flower in full sun to part shade in moist or boggy soil. It tolerates some flooding, but not drought.
Foliage and flowers: The bronze-green leaves are oval with tiny toothed edges. In winter the plant dies down to a basal rosette. In midsummer, each stem produces a raceme about 1 foot long covered with tubular scarlet-red flowers.
Care: Cardinal flower is susceptible to rust, smut, and leaf spots. To prevent, keep plants healthy, clear dead plant debris from the base of plants, mulch with organic material, and plant where air circulation is good.
Propagation: Plant seeds or separate the basal offshoots in spring. It self-sows.
Noteworthy plants: 'Alba' has white flowers. 'Angel Song' blooms with salmon and cream flowers. For truly deep red flowers, choose 'Ruby Slippers'.

Lysimachia nummularia
Creeping Jenny, moneywort

- **Hardiness zones: 4–8**
- **Heat zones: 8–1**
- **Light: Full sun to part shade**
- **Size: 2"H×indefinite spread**
- **Features: Spreading groundcover**

Creeping Jenny is an evergreen groundcover that spreads rapidly and works as an oxygenator in the pond. It is easy to weed out, but it may be too invasive for small ponds.

Siting: Grow it in full sun to part shade in moist, rich soil in bogs or at the water's edge. It can grow in as much as 2 inches of water, although it also tolerates dry soil conditions.

Foliage and flowers: The ¾-inch leaves are round to ovate, and heart-shaped at the base. Cup-shape yellow flowers blossom in spring.

Care: No special care is required.

Propagation: Sow seed or divide plants. Creeping jenny will easily root at the stem nodes, and even a tiny piece will spread rapidly.

Noteworthy plants: *L. nummularia* 'Aurea' (golden creeping Jenny) has gold-colored leaves that light up garden space.

Golden creeping Jenny, *L. nummularia* 'Aurea'

Myosotis scorpioides
Water forget-me-not

- **Hardiness zones: 5–9**
- **Heat zones: 9–5**
- **Light: Sun or part shade**
- **Size: 1'H×1'W**
- **Features: Delicate sprays of blue flowers**

Water forget-me-not, *M. scorpioides*

Also known as true forget-me-not, this water-loving creeper is truly unforgettable with its sprays of sky blue flowers.

Siting: Grow water forget-me-not in sun or part shade along the margin of a pond or in an aquatic container no more than 4 inches under water. With its widespread matted root system, it is considered an invasive plant in many states.

Foliage and flowers: Sky blue, flat flowers ⅜-inch-across—each with a white, pink, or yellow eye—unfold in a "fiddleneck" fashion on open cymes in the early summer.

Care: Protect the water forget-me-not from slugs and snails.

Propagation: Sow seed in situ (it self-sows readily) or divide the plant in the early spring.

Noteworthy plants: *M. scorpioides* 'Semperflorens' is a dwarf variety only 8 inches tall.

Pontederia cordata
Pickerel weed

- **Hardiness zones: 3–11**
- **Heat zones: 12–1**
- **Light: Full sun**
- **Size: 2–3'H×3'W**
- **Features: Blue flower spikes**

Erect, lance-shaped, glossy foliage that rises on stems high above the water surface and spikes of funnel-shape, blue or purple flowers on stiff stems make pickerel weed a distinctive pond plant.

Siting: Plant in full sun in fertile, loamy soil at the edge of a pond or in up to 3 inches of water.

Foliage and flowers: Large, glossy leaves that are broadly ovate stand erect above the water. Some leaves also are submerged or float on the water surface. Blue delphinium-like flower spikes bloom from spring to early autumn.

Care: If spider mites are a problem, introduce predatory mites, which are available at garden centers.

Propagation: Divide in late spring when growth starts.

Noteworthy plants: 'Alba' is slightly more compact and has ice-white flowers.

Pickerel weed, *P. cordata*

Sagittaria sagittifolia
Japanese arrowhead

- Hardiness zones: 5–11
- Heat zones: 12–5
- Light: Full sun
- Size: 36"H×indefinite spread
- Features: Arrowhead-shaped leaves, white flowers

Japanese arrowhead, *S. sagittifolia*

Distinctive, arrowhead-shape leaves characterize this aquatic tuber that produces whirled racemes of white flowers in summer.

Siting: Plant in very moist soil or in water no more than 3-6 inches deep in full sun.

Foliage and flowers: The plant's common name comes from its arrowhead-shaped leaves. When grown in deep water, Japanese arrowhead grows long, ribbon-like leaves that float on the surface. In summer it produces racemes of single white flowers on stalks up to 36 inches long.

Care: Arrowhead can be invasive; in earth-bottom ponds, grow it in containers.

Propagation: Divide clumps or plant runners in the spring. Sow seed in trays of shallow water when they are ripe.

Noteworthy plants: The flowers of the double form of Japanese arrowhead, 'Flore Pleno', look like fluffy snowballs; this is harder to establish than the single form. Another species, *S. latifolia*, grows 18–36 inches tall with a 36-inch spread.

Thalia dealbata
Hardy canna, thalia

- Hardiness zones: 6–11
- Heat zones: 12–6
- Light: Full sun
- Size: 6–10'H×6'W
- Features: Violet flowers carried high above foliage

Standing tall above the water, handsome, canna-like, blue-green leaves make this plant a dramatic specimen in a medium to large pond, adding a tropical effect. Violet flowers bloom at the end of long, fishing pole-like stalks.

Siting: Plant thalia at the edge of a sunny pond in up to 3 inches of water. Give thalia plenty of room for the 6-foot spread.

Foliage and flowers: Thick ovate sage-green leaves are dusted with white powder and edged in purple. Small violet flowers bloom in summer on 8-inch long panicles at the end of long stalks. Bees love the flowers.

Care: Grow hardy canna in a suitably large container of at least 5 gallons. Apply a balanced aquatic fertilizer monthly in summer. If you observe leaf-rolling caterpillars eating the foliage, apply *Bacillus thuringiensis* (Bt).

Propagation: Divide in spring.

Noteworthy plants: There are no named cultivars.

Hardy canna, *T. dealbata*

Zantedeschia aethiopica
Calla lily

- Hardiness zones: 8–10
- Heat zones: 10–4
- Light: Full sun to part shade
- Size: 16"H×24"W
- Features: Glossy bright green leaves, elegant white flowers

Calla lily, *Z. aethiopica* 'Green Goddess'

The calla lily is a South African native that will grow in standing water and also tolerate drought. The dramatic white spathes with a distinctive, pokerlike yellow spadix bloom from spring through summer, making calla lilies worth overwintering indoors where they are not hardy.

Siting: Grow in moist soil in full sun or part shade, or in a 10–12-inch wide aquatic container filled with heavy soil in water up to 3 inches deep.

Foliage and flowers: Rising above the glossy arrow-shaped foliage, eye-catching, horn-shaped white spathes surround a pokerlike, central yellow spadix from spring through summer. It is an excellent cut flower, lasting a long time in water.

Care: In cold climates, overwinter plants indoors.

Propagation: Divide in spring.

Noteworthy plants: The hybrid 'Crowborough' is somewhat hardier than the species. 'Green Goddess' has white spathes with green streaks.

FLOATING PLANTS

Drawing their nutrients from the water, floating plants are valuable for oxygenating and keeping pond water clear, as well as providing shade and protection for fish. Their roots protrude into the water and need no soil at all. Most are rapid growers (and even proclaimed as weeds in some countries and states), and need to be controlled. Before ordering any from a catalog, check your state for local regulations regarding possession of these plants.

Azolla filiculoides
Fairy moss

- **Hardiness Zones: 7–11**
- **Heat Zones: 12–1**
- **Light: Full sun to part shade**
- **Size: ⅛"H × indefinite spread**
- **Features: Lacy foliage**

The fernlike foliage of azolla measures about ½ inch across. Considered a weedy menace in some states, only grow fairy moss in small ponds where you can easily remove the excess growth with a net.
Siting: Float fairy moss on the water surface in full sun or part shade.
Foliage and flowers: Tiny, delicate, lacy foliage that resembles a miniature fern frond is light green with reddish markings. There are no flowers.
Care: Where it is not hardy, overwinter fairy moss in a frost-free spot in a jar of moist soil.
Propagation: A rampant spreader, small bunches of fairy moss scattered on the water surface will quickly multiply.
Noteworthy plants: Another species, *A. pinnata*, is cold hardy in Zones 8–10. It has more feathery, slender foliage than *A. filiculoides*.

Fairy moss, *A. filiculoides*

Eichhornia crassipes
Water hyacinth

- **Hardiness zones: 9–11**
- **Heat zones: 12–1**
- **Light: Full sun**
- **Size: 18"H × 18"W**
- **Features: Showy blue flowers**

Water hyacinth, *E. crassipes*

Considered a weed in African and southern United States wetlands, the 12-inch-long purplish root masses of water hyacinth provide an ideal fish spawning ground. It is a great filtering plant. Illegal in many southern states, water hyacinth should only be grown in contained ponds and should not be grown near waterways.
Siting: Float in ponds in full sun.
Foliage and flowers: Rosettes of rounded or ovate leaves float on the surface. Showy lavender-blue flowers bloom on 12-inch stalks that stand above the water in summer.
Care: Where not hardy, overwinter water hyacinth indoors with plenty of light and air temperature of about 59°F.
Propagation: New plants will grow from a detatched offshoot at any time of year.
Noteworthy plants: There are no hybridized cultivars. These plants are considered one of the worst weeds in the world. They can choke natural waterways. Do not allow them to escape into the wild.

Hydrocharis morsus-ranae
Frogbit

- **Hardiness zones: 6–11**
- **Heat zones: 12–7**
- **Light: Full sun**
- **Size: 1–2"H × indefinite spread**
- **Features: Round floating leaves and small white flowers**

Frogbit is a good choice for a small pond because the foliage is like miniature water lily pads; however, if it escapes into natural bodies of water, it can grow rampantly, choking out other natural vegetation. It is illegal in some states, so check for local regulations.
Siting: Grown in shallow, alkaline water in full sun, it readily takes root in soil.
Foliage and flowers: Rosettes of rounded, glossy mid-green leaves float on the water surface. A succession of papery ¾-inch white flowers with a yellow spot at the base bloom in summer.
Care: Frogbit requires no special care, although the foliage may be damaged by water snails. Deciduous in autumn, the plant overwinters at the bottom of the pond in dormant buds.
Propagation: Divide clumps in spring or summer
Noteworthy plants: There are no named cultivars of frogbit.

Frogbit, *H. morsus-ranae*

Lemna minor
Lesser duckweed

- **Hardiness zones: 3–11**
- **Heat zones: 12–1**
- **Light: Full sun**
- **Size: 1–2"H × indefinite spread**
- **Features: Tiny foliage covers pond**

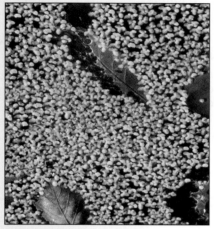

Lesser duckweed, *L. minor*

Although a vigorous spreader, nutrient-rich duckweed provides food for fish and waterfowl, and shades the water surface, reducing algae growth. It also is a natural biofilter.
Siting: Grow lesser duckweed on the water surface. Even if you don't plant it, you'll probably find it in your pond sooner or later, introduced on the leaves or stems of another pond plant.
Foliage and flowers: Tiny floating foliage can cover any fresh body of water in a solid green mat-covering surface. Considered the world's smallest flowering plant, its flowers are inconspicuous and rare. Duckweed is grown for foliage and its benefits to ponds.
Care: Lesser duckweed prefers cool temperatures and may disappear in hot summers.
Propagation: This plant multiplies prolifically. However, it is easy to scoop out any excess. A single plant can reproduce itself about every three days in nutrient-rich waters. Use excess plants as mulch in your garden.
Noteworthy plants: There are no hybridized cultivars.

Pistia stratiotes
Water lettuce

- **Hardiness zones: 9–11**
- **Heat zones: 12–4**
- **Light: Full sun with midday shade**
- **Size: 4"H × indefinite spread**
- **Features: Nicely textured leaves**

The feathery roots, which change color through the season from white to purple, and finally darkening to black, are a haven for spawning fish.
Siting: Float water lettuce on the water surface in full sun, ideally with some midday shade. Water lettuce is a heat lover.
Foliage and flowers: This plant has wedge-shape, felted, crinkled leaves that float on the water in rosettes. The flowers are insignificant and green.
Care: Where it is not hardy, overwinter it indoors at a minimum of 50°F. Return the plant outdoors when the weather is consistently warm, in late spring.
Propagation: Divide clumps any time in summer.
Noteworthy plants: For a denser cluster of foliage, choose the cultivar 'Rosette'.

Water lettuce, *P. stratiotes*

Utricularia gibba
Humped bladderwort

- **Hardiness zones: 3–10**
- **Heat zones: 12–10**
- **Light: Full sun**
- **Size: 2"H × 8"W**
- **Features: Yellow flowers similar to snapdragons**

Humped bladderwort, *U. gibba*

This plant is nicknamed bladderwort because of pear-shape bladders that open abruptly when trigger hairs are disturbed; it sucks in water and any aquatic insect responsible for setting off the trap. When digestion is complete, special cells extract the nutrient-rich water from the bladder into the stem, thereby restoring the vacuum and resetting the trap.
Siting: Grow in full sun.
Foliage and flowers: Humped bladderwort has slender stems with feathery, threadlike leaf segments up to 3 inches long. Attached along these leaves are the carnivorous bladders. Clusters of red-vein yellow flowers resembling snapdragons stand above the water on 8-inch-tall stalks in midsummer.
Care: No special care is required.
Propagation: Replant any buds that sink to the bottom of the pond after flowering or divide mats of foliage in summer.
Noteworthy plants: There are no hybridized cultivars.

Ceratophyllum demersum
Hornwort

- **Hardiness zones: 6–9**
- **Heat zones: 9–6**
- **Light: Full sun**
- **Size: Indefinite spread**
- **Features: Bottlebrush-like foliage**

Easy to grow, hornwort is an excellent submerged plant. Whorls of dark-green, foliage resemble bottlebrushes. The plants overwinter as dormant buds on the pond bottom.
Siting: Hornwort grows best in full sun in water 24–36 inches deep. It tolerates some shade.
Foliage and flowers: Stiff olive-green to almost black leaves are sometimes coated with lime, giving them a crunchy feel. Tiny flowers shaped like cups bloom in summer.
Care: No special care required.
Propagation: Anchor cuttings in sand topped with pea gravel.
Noteworthy plants: There are no hybridized cultivars.

Hornwort, C. demersum

Myriophyllum verticillatum
Whorled milfoil

- **Hardiness zones: 3–11**
- **Heat zones: 12–1**
- **Light: Full sun**
- **Size: 3'H × indefinite spread**
- **Features: Feathery foliage**

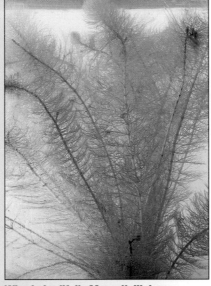

Whorled milfoil, M. verticillatum

Decorative, fine, feathery foliage grows along trailing, submerged stems. Milfoil is excellent for providing shelter for fish, giving them hiding places among its leaves, as well as oxygenating the water.
Siting: Plant water milfoil in full sun in loam-filled containers sunk 3 feet deep in water.
Foliage and flowers: Each leaf is featherlike and consists of paired leaflets. The leaves on the flower stalks above the water are located below each flower and are much smaller than the underwater leaves, although they are larger than the flowers. In summer, 6-inch-long spikes of yellowish flowers protrude just above the water surface; however they are small and not showy.
Care: Winter-damaged top growth will renew in spring.
Propagation: Take cuttings in spring or summer.
Noteworthy plants: There are no hybridized cultivars.

Ranunculus aquatilis
Water buttercup, water crowfoot

- **Hardiness zones: 5–8**
- **Heat zones: 8–5**
- **Light: Full sun**
- **Size: Indefinite spread**
- **Features: White flowers with yellow centers**

One of the few flowering submerged plants, water buttercup is excellent in ponds of any size because it dies back on its own after flowering, and thus never becomes invasive.
Siting: Grow water buttercup in still or moving water that is 6–24 inches deep in full sun.
Foliage and flowers: Underwater foliage is hair-like; the surface foliage is rounded or kidney-shape and divided into lobes resembling clover leaves. In late spring and early summer, water buttercup produces cupped flowers ¾-inch across with white petals and yellow centers rising from the water's surface.
Care: No special care is required.
Propagation: Take cuttings in spring or summer.
Noteworthy plants: There are no hybridized cultivars.

Water buttercup, R. aquatilis

DEEP-WATER PLANTS

Deep-water plants have their roots in submerged pots (or in the soil of an earth-bottom pond) and their leaves floating on the water surface. Flowers either float or stand on stalks above the water. Their leaves help to keep the water clear and provide cooling shade for the fish.

Aponogeton distachyos
Water hawthorn

- **Hardiness zones: 9–10**
- **Heat zones: 12–10**
- **Light: Full sun**
- **Size: Floats on surface; 4'W**
- **Features: Fragrant flowers**

Water hawthorn, *A. distachyos*

Water hawthorn is easy to grow and has long-lasting, fragrant flowers. The elongated, oblong leaves are evergreen in mild winters.
Siting: Plant 1–3 feet deep in full sun. Water hawthorn will tolerate some shade and moving water. The deeper it is planted, the more cold-hardy it will be.
Foliage and flowers: In the winter and spring, vanilla-scented white flowers float on the water.
Care: Remove dead foliage in the autumn; prune to 1–2 inches above the soil line. Algae may smother young leaves.
Propagation: Divide in late spring.
Noteworthy plants: There are no hybridized cultivars.

Hydrocleys nymphoides
Water poppy

- **Hardiness zones: 9–10**
- **Heat zones: 10–7**
- **Light: Full sun**
- **Size: Floats on water; indefinite spread**
- **Features: Yellow flowers float on the surface**

The water poppy is a tropical water plant with small heart-shape leaves and yellow flowers that float on the surface.
Siting: Plant it in full sun in submerged containers or in soil of earth-bottom ponds up to 9 inches deep. Water poppy prefers rich topsoil.
Foliage and flowers: This plant flowers profusely in the spring and summer with yellow blossoms that resemble California poppies. The olive-green, heart-shaped leaves and yellow flowers float on the water's surface.
Care: Where not hardy, bring the plants indoors before the first frost. They will overwinter successfully in a shallow tub as long as they get plenty of water and light.
Propagation: Divide young plants in spring.
Noteworthy plants: There are no named cultivars.

Water poppy, *H. nymphoides*

Ludwigia sedioides
Mosaic plant

- **Hardiness zones: 11–15**
- **Heat zones: 12–10**
- **Light: Full sun or dappled shade**
- **Size: 2–18"H×24"W in a single season**
- **Features: Diamond-shape leaves and cup-shape flowers**

Mosaic plant, *L. sedioides*

A tropical plant, mosaic plant is grown as an annual in cooler climates.
Siting: Grow mosaic plant in full sun or dappled shade with the crown submerged 12–18 inches underwater. It prefers warm, acidic water and will die if the water pH reaches 8 or higher.
Foliage and flowers: Diamond-shape, soft green, sometimes maroon-tinged leaves float on the water surface in a mosaic pattern. Cup-shape bright yellow flowers blossom in late summer and autumn.
Care: In the autumn, prune mosaic plant to 1–2 inches above the soil line. In zones colder than Zone 8, overwinter indoors in an aquarium with water warmer than 70°F. Add supplemental light, and keep the water pH neutral to acidic.
Propagation: Divide the plant in the spring.
Noteworthy plants: There are no named cultivars.

Marsilea mutica
Water clover

- **Hardiness zones: 6–11**
- **Heat zones: 12–6**
- **Light: Full sun**
- **Size: Floats on water surface; unlimited spread**
- **Features: Tricolor foliage**

Water clover, *M. mutica*

Actually an aquatic fern native to Australia, water clover resembles a four-leaf clover. It makes an excellent transition plant for the edge of a pond and also provides good shade for fish.

Siting: Grow water clover in full sun along the margin of a pond or in an aquatic container 6–12 inches below the water surface. This plant is invasive in earth-bottom ponds.

Foliage and flowers: Water clover is grown for its colorful foliage. Each quartet of 3-inch leaves has two shades of green with a thin maroon margin. The color pattern is akin to a pansy's face.

Care: Prune away any yellowing foliage as it occurs.

Propagation: Separate individual plantlets from the stems, or take cuttings to make new plants.

Noteworthy plants: There are no named cultivars.

Nymphoides cristata
Water snowflake

- **Hardiness zones: 7–11**
- **Heat zones: 12–7**
- **Light: Full sun or part shade**
- **Size: Floats on water surface; indefinite spread**
- **Features: Mottled leaves and white flowers**

The 3-inch-diameter, mottled red and green, heart-shaped leaves float on the water surface. Do not let it escape into the wild as it reproduces vigorously and is considered a noxious weed in many states.

Siting: Grow water snowflake in full sun or part shade in water 3–12 inches deep.

Foliage and flowers: The oval yellow-green leaves are mottled with reddish-brown markings. Plentiful clusters of white, fragrant, crested flowers, ¾-inch across, bloom from spring through autumn.

Care: Water snowflake requires no special care.

Propagation: Water snowflake reproduces rapidly by producing plantlets near the top of each stem, just beneath the leaf. Each new plant develops its own roots and leaves.

Noteworthy plants: There are no hybridized cultivars.

Water snowflake, *N. cristata*

Nymphoides peltata
Yellow floating heart

- **Hardiness zones: 6–11**
- **Heat zones: 12–6**
- **Light: Full sun**
- **Size: Floats on water surface; indefinite spread**
- **Features: Heart-shape leaves and yellow flowers**

Yellow floating heart, *N. peltata*

Because it is a rapid spreader, yellow floating heart is useful to give water cover while water lilies are becoming established.

Siting: Grow yellow floating heart in full sun in water less than 6–12 inches deep.

Foliage and flowers: Floating, heart-shape leaves 2 inches across look like miniature water lilies. One-inch funnel-shape buttercup yellow flowers, each with five fringed petals, open in groups of two to five on stalks above the water in the summer.

Care: Weed out excess plants if it spreads out of control. It is a potential weed when introduced into the wild.

Propagation: Yellow floating heart spreads by water-dispersed seeds and stolons. Broken-off leaves with part of a stem will also form new plants.

Noteworthy plants: There are no hybridized cultivars.

Nymphaea
Hardy water lily

- Hardiness zones: 3–11
- Heat zones: 12–1
- Light: Full sun
- Size: Varies with hybrid from 2–18'W
- Features: Beautiful flowers

Water lilies are the queens of the pond garden, valued not only for their beautiful flowers, but also for their attractive, sometimes mottled, and often textured flat leaves and their role in pond health. The floating foliage shades the pond, thus slowing the growth of unwanted algae and providing respite to fish from the hot sun.

Water lilies are divided into two categories: hardy varieties that can take temperatures as cold as −40°F and tropicals that require a frost-free environment.
Siting: Grow water lilies in full sun in still water. Do not plant them near waterfalls that churn up the water. In hardiness Zones 10 and 11, you can plant water lilies year round. In other zones, plant hardy lilies any time during the growing season once the danger of frost is past. The sooner you get them in, however, the sooner you'll be able to enjoy their blooms.

Water lily, *N.* 'Perry's Opal Fire'

In any climate, the ideal water depth depends on the plant size. Start at a depth where the leaves can float. As the plant grows, increase the depth, keeping the leaves comfortably floating on the surface. Water lily containers can be as shallow as 6–8 inches, but these plants need a pot that's a minimum of 12–18 inches in diameter. Vigorous growers need even wider pots. Larger containers mean dividing the plant less

Water lily, *N.* 'Colorado'

often, but they are more unwieldy to move.
Foliage and flowers: Broad, round or ovate leaves, called pads, float on the water surface. Many are mottled, edged, or variegated with shades of red or brown. Hardy lily blooms come in a wide array of sizes, colors, and forms. Colors include varying shades of yellow, pink, red, and white. They may be doubles or singles, cup-shape or star-shape. They flower continually from spring through autumn, opening around 9 a.m. and closing in late afternoon between 3 and 5 p.m.
Care: Remove dead foliage as it appears, and deadhead spent flowers. Fertilize monthly with commercially available pellets in spring and fall, and biweekly during the midsummer flowering season. Divide in the spring every 2–3 years (possibly

annually in the South) or when the lily pads start to stand above the water. Hardy lilies can overwinter in the pond if the roots don't freeze. If the pond will completely freeze, remove the containers from the water, wrap the containers in plastic bags to keep the soil moist, and store them in a cool place, such as a shed or garage.
Propagation: In spring, unearth the rhizome, rinse off the soil, and then cut it into 3–6-inch long sections, making sure to have a growing tip with each division, and replant.
Noteworthy plants: 'Colorado': free flowering salmon or apricot-pink blossoms stand 5–6 inches above the water surface; mottled leaves; spreads 9–18 feet. 'Joey Tomocik': 5–6-inch vibrant lemon-yellow flowers; spreads 6–12 feet; quick to reestablish in spring; flowers in partial shade. 'Perry's Opal Fire': 5–6-inch rich pink, peony-shape, double, fragrant flowers; free flowering; 7–10-inch green leaves; new leaves are purplish-red; spreads 6–12 feet. 'Perry's Baby Red': dwarf water lily good for tub or small pond; 3-inch deep red flowers with a slight fragrance; 4–6-inch green leaves; new leaves are purple; free flowering.

Water lily, *N.* 'Joey Tomocik'

Nymphaea
Tropical water lily

- **Hardiness zones: 10–11**
- **Heat zones: 12–7**
- **Light: Full sun**
- **Size: Ranges from 2–18'W**
- **Features: Beautiful, often fragrant flowers**

Water lily, *Nymphaea* spp.

Tropical water lilies may be night or day bloomers. They are valued for their potent scent.
Siting: Grow tropical water lilies in full sun in still water, away from waterfalls. In hardiness Zones 10 and 11, you can plant water lilies year round. Wait until the water has warmed to 60°F before planting tropical water lilies. In any climate, the ideal water depth depends on the plant size. Start at a depth where the leaves can float. As the plant grows, lower the depth, keeping the leaves comfortably floating on the surface. Containers can be as shallow as 6–8 inches, but they must be at least 12–18 inches in diameter. Vigorous growers need even more width.

Water lily, *N.* 'Albert Greenberg'

Foliage and flowers: Broad, round or ovate leaves, called pads, float on the water surface. Many are mottled, edged, or variegated with shades of red or brown. Tropicals grow in all the colors of hardy water lilies, plus shades of blue and purple. Day-flowering tropicals open in the morning and close at dusk. The night-bloomers open at dusk and close late the following morning. Tropical varieties produce more flowers and are more fragrant than the hardies; however they need daytime heat to bloom and do not perform well in cool regions.
Care: Remove dead foliage as it develops, and deadhead spent flowers. Fertilize monthly with aquatic plant pellets in spring and fall, and during the flowering season. Divide in spring every two to three years (possibly annually in the South) or when the lily pads start to stand above the water. In cold regions, unearth the bulbs to overwinter them indoors. (See instructions on page 84.)
Propagation: In spring, unearth the bulb, rinse off the soil, and replant. Some tropical lilies are viviparous, developing perfectly formed baby plants on their leaves. Pull off the new plants and pot in garden soil. Set the pot in water at a depth where the leaves float on the surface.
Noteworthy plants: Among the night-blooming possibilities, 'Wood's White Knight' is a

Water lily, *N.* 'Texas Shell Pink'

prolific bloomer with vanilla, star-shape semi-double flowers with lemon-tipped stamens. The flowers stand tall above scalloped emerald leaves that are variegated underneath. It spreads 6–12 feet. 'Emily Grant Hutchings' is another profuse bloomer with 7-inch, coral-pink, star-shape, semidouble flowers. It adjusts well to tubs or other containers and will flower in the winter if sheltered in a greenhouse. It spreads 6–12 feet. 'Texas Shell Pink' has soft pink flowers, and wavy edge, bronze-green foliage. It spreads

Water lily, *N.* 'Emily Grant Hutchings'

6–12 feet. 'Red Flare' has fragrant, 10-inch vermillion flowers with deep-maroon stamens. The flowers stand 12 inches tall above mahogany foliage with crimped edges. It spreads 5–6 feet. Among day-blooming plants consider 'Panama Pacific', which has fragrant, 5-inch, star-shape deep-purple flowers with purple-tip yellow stamens. It blooms profusely above rich bronze foliage with green veins. A viviparous variety, it spreads only 3–12 feet, making it suitable for containers. 'William McLane' blossoms over a long season with blue flowers with blue-tipped yellow stamens. It spreads 6–12 feet. 'Albert Greenberg' has speckled foliage that spreads 6–12 feet. Its rose-tip apricot flowers open 6–7 inches across.

Nelumbo lutea
American lotus

N. nucifera
Sacred lotus

- **Hardiness zones: 4–11**
- **Heat zones: 12–3**
- **Light: Full sun**
- **Size: 2–6'H × indefinite spread**
- **Features: Flowers and ornamental seed heads**

Large, almost circular leaves held above the water, plus waxy single or double flowers in midsummer through autumn and distinctive seed pods make lotuses a dramatic focal point in a pond. However, they are extremely invasive in an earth-bottom pond. Once you plant them in that environment, even in containers, you'll have a very difficult time eradicating them.
Siting: Plant each tuber in full sun in a large round container at least 18 inches in diameter and 9 inches deep. Place the tub 16–24 inches deep for large specimens, 6–9 inches deep for smaller ones. They will accept as little as 2–4 inches of water over the container.
Foliage and flowers: Large round, slightly concave leaves are bluish or grayish green. Once they have baked for several weeks in sunny weather above 80ºF, fragrant blossoms in colors ranging from yellow (*N. lutea*),

Sacred lotus, *N.* 'Charles Thomas'

pink, or white (*N. nucifera*) to a range of hybridized shades of pinks, reds, and whites open and close early in the morning the first day, open from mid-morning to noon the second, and again in mid-morning the third day, with the petals dropping by mid-afternoon to reveal the round seed pod that resembles a brown kiwi fruit sliced in half.

American lotus, *N.* 'Chawan Basu'

Care: Lotus are heavy feeders; add five or six pellets of aquatic plant fertilizer once several leaves have emerged, and then feed monthly until about a month before your first frost date. Remove fading foliage on a regular basis. If your pond freezes in the winter, remove the container from the water and store it wrapped in a plastic bag in a cool, frost-free spot.
Propagation: Collect and save ripe seed from dried pods. In early spring, nick the hard seed and drop in water. They should germinate in 10–20 days. Plant seedlings in soil once the third leaf has appeared. Carefully divide fragile tubers (they resent disturbance) in early spring.
Noteworthy plants: For smaller cultivars, choose from the following: 'Charles Thomas' is an 18–36-inch tall plant with 6–8-inch single pink flowers with a hint of lavender and the scent of anise. 'Chawan Basu' grows 18–36 inches tall and has

Dwarf lotus, *N.* 'Momo Botan'

single cream-color flowers edged with pink. Both are well suited to barrels and containers. Lotus 'Momo Botan' grows 18–36 inches tall with leaves that are 12–18 inches in diameter. Its deep rose double flowers with yellow centers are 6 inches across. It is ideal for small ponds or whiskey barrels. 'Mrs. Perry D. Slocum' is a large hybrid that grows 5–7 feet tall. It produces dramatic 12-inch double blossoms with a strong anise scent. Over a period of days, the flowers change color from pink to creamy yellow.

Lotus, *N.* 'Mrs. Perry D. Slocum'

GLOSSARY

Aerator: A device for introducing air into a body of water.

Air stone: Called by many names, including aeration stone and air diffuser stone, this device creates tiny oxygen bubbles that rise to the surface of the water. The air bubbles bring the bottom water to the surface where the water grabs oxygen from the atmosphere and circulates it in the pond.

Anaerobic bacteria: Bacteria that can live and grow without atmospheric oxygen. These bacteria grow in the airless atmosphere created by decaying plant material at the bottom of a pond, and can produce gases that are deadly to fish. To tell if you have a dangerous situation for your fish, stir up the bottom sediment and smell the rising bubbles. A distinct sulfur odor indicates a problem. For the solution, *see* Air stone.

Biofilter: A device that converts toxic impurities in the water (primarily ammonia from fish waste) to benign substances by using beneficial bacteria.

Bog: Areas where the water table is high so that the ground is naturally moist, but the plants are not constantly in standing water. Generally the soil is highly acidic and low in oxygen and nutrients.

Catch basin: A container or chamber designed to collect water.

Charcoal/carbon filter: A device containing an activated charcoal/carbon pouch through which the water is drawn to purify it. Algicides and other chemicals may be added for additional pond care.

Chloramine: A combination of ammonia and chlorine that is added to many municipal water supplies instead of free chlorine. Chloramine is many times more toxic to fish than chlorine and does not dissipate rapidly from water. If you have fish or other pond creatures, you will have to take steps to remove it.

Cyme: A determinate, branched arrangement of flowers on a single stem with a flat or rounded top, such as *Asclepias incarnata* (swamp milkweed).

Filamentous algae: Also known as pond scum or hair algae, a free-floating plant that does not have true leaves, stems, or roots.

▲ A fountain makes a dramatic focal point when combined with trees, shrubs, and colorful perennials.

It will be present at some level in all ponds and is an important food source for protozoa and small fish.

Flexible liner: A pond liner made of waterproof, flexible material such as polyethylene, PVC, or synthetic rubber. Polyethylene is the least durable, lasting only 2–3 years. PVC has a life span of 10–15 years. The most expensive and most durable flexible liner material is synthetic rubber, either ethylene propylene diene monomer (EPDM) or butyl.

Floating plant: A plant that grows with its roots submerged in water and its leaves and stems free-floating on the surface; also known as a "floater."

GFCI or GFI: A ground fault circuit interrupter (GFCI) or ground fault interrupter (GFI) provides protection against power overloads, short circuits, and ground faults (current leaks). If it detects even low levels of electrical current leaks, it shuts off the power, preventing serious shock. They are required on electrical outlets located outdoors and in areas that are exposed to moisture.

Head: The pressure that must be generated by a pond pump to run a waterfall, fountain, or other pond component. The pond pump must be capable of lifting the required volume of water to a certain head or height.

Header pool: The top pond in a series of ponds situated at different levels and connected by waterfalls or cascades.

Intake filter: A device to screen debris from getting into a submersible pump and fountain nozzle. *See also* Prefilter.

Koi: Fancy, brightly colored carp *(Cyprinus carpio)* native to Japan and eastern Asia. In Japan the ornamental varieties so prized in fish ponds are properly called *Nishikigoi,* which means brocaded carp.

Lift: *See* Head.

Marginal plant: A plant that grows in the shallow water at the edge of a pond. The roots are submerged in water, and the leaves and flowers stand above the water surface. Many marginal plants are quite invasive, particularly when planted along the edges of earth-bottom ponds. To avoid them taking over, grow marginal plants in submerged baskets.

Mechanical filter: A device that mechanically removes debris or detritus from the air or water, typically a sieve.

Muriatic acid: An industrial-strength solution of hydrogen chloride gas dissolved in water, also known as hydrochloric acid. It is used for heavy-duty masonry cleaning, preparation of masonry for painting or sealing, and removal of mineral deposits.

Orfe: An orange, freshwater fish, sometimes with black dots on its head and back, belonging to the carp family. This is a sociable, schooling species, so release at least five individuals for best results. Active by nature, orfes tend to stay near the water surface, making them fun to watch.

Panicle: A branched group of flowers in which each branch has its own cluster of flowers (raceme), making a feathery effect. Astilbe is an example.

Pea gravel: Gravel that approximates the size of peas.

Plant filter: A system that keeps ponds clean by using plants to extract impurities from the water.

Prefilter: A device used with submersible pumps to strain large debris to prevent it from getting caught in the pump. *See also* Intake filter.

Preformed liner: A rigid structure made of molded plastic or fiberglass to be used as a pond foundation.

Raceme: An inflorescence or cluster of flowers arranged singly along an elongated, unbranched stem, such as the cardinal flower *(Lobelia cardinalis).*

Rigid liner: *See* Preformed liner.

Scavenger: A water creature, such as an aquatic snail or tadpole, that helps control algae in a garden pool.

Solvent cement: A mixture of plastic resins, solvents, and other additives used to permanently bond multiple pieces of plastic into one section.

Spill stone: A flat stone that water can run over, usually from an upper to a lower pond or basin.

Spillway: A channel for water overflow, such as from a pond or spa.

Submerged plant: A plant that lives completely under the water. Any flowers appear on or above the surface. It releases oxygen into the water as well as absorbs minerals and carbon dioxide, thus helping to starve the algae and promote a balanced aquatic environment. In addition, submerged plants provide food and shelter for fish.

Terrace: A raised bank of earth having vertical or sloping sides and a flat top.

Underlayment: A layer of material installed between the ground and pond liner to prevent punctures from rough or rocky ground. Made of a permeable material (old carpet, newspapers, and geotextile fabric are all possibilities).

UV clarifier: An electronic fixture that uses ultraviolet light to kill suspended algae and ensure clear pond water.

Viviparous: The ability of a plant to produce "baby" plants on a mature leaf.

Watercourse: The path followed by a constructed stream.

Water-permeable: Anything that water can pass through or penetrate.

GARDEN POOL RESOURCES

Complete Providers - Carry a full line of pond-related products to build and stock a home water feature.
Equipment - Hard goods used to build a water feature.
Fish
Membership Organizations
Miscellaneous
Plants
Publications
Supplies - Consumable items, such as water-treatment chemicals, plant fertilizers, and fish food.
Note: To make this list easier to use, resources have been listed under their primary product. But most companies carry other products as well, which are described.

Complete providers

BECKETT WATER GARDENING
5931 Campus Circle Dr. W
Irving, TX 75063-2606
888/BECKETT
www.888beckett.com
Complete line of water gardening products, no fish or plants. Wholesale only; on-line catalog; informative website.

GILBERG PERENNIAL FARMS
2906 Ossenfort Rd.
Wildwood, MO 63038
636/458-2033
info@gilbergfarms.com
www.gilbergperennials.com
Complete line of water gardening supplies, including plants and fish. Troubleshooting and consultation. No mail order; visit retail shop. Call for hours.

LILYPONS WATER GARDENS
6800 Lilypons Rd.
Adamstown, MD 21710
800/999-LILY
www.lilypons.com
email: info@lilypons.com
One-stop shop for equipment, supplies, fish, plants, and accessories. Visit retail shop, or order on-line or from catalog. Installation, cleaning, and maintenance.

PARADISE WATER GARDENS
14 May St.
Whitman, MA 02382-1841
800/955-0161
www.paradisewatergardens.com
Everything necessary to build and stock ponds.

S. SCHERER & SONS, INC.
104 Waterside Rd.
Northport, NY 11768
631/261-7432
www.waterlilyfarm.com
Fourth-generation aquatic nursery. Everything to build and supply water gardens, including fish and 200 varieties of plants. Visit retail shop, or order on-line or from catalog.

VAN NESS WATER GARDENS
2460 N. Euclid Ave.
Upland, CA 91784-1199
800/205-2425
www.vnwg.com
Equipment, fish, and plants. Informative website and catalog.

WATERFORD GARDENS
74 E. Allendale Rd.
Saddle River, NJ 07458
201/327-0721
email: splash@waterfordgardens.com
www.waterfordgardens.com
Complete provider. Installation and maintenance. Visit retail shop or order on-line or from catalog.

Equipment

AL ZIMMER'S PONDS & SUPPLIES
6271 Perkiomen Ave.
Birdsboro, PA 19508
800/722-8877
email: AZPonds@aol.com
www.azponds.com
Equipment and supplies.

AQUA ART POND SPECIALISTS
11-F Poco Way, Suite 154
American Canyon, CA 94503
800/995-9164 (Order line)
707/642-7663 (Help line)
www.aquaart.com
Equipment and accessories.

AQUATIC ECO-SYSTEMS, INC.
2395 Apopka Blvd.
Apopka, FL 32703
877/347-4788
www.aquaticeco.com
Equipment, supplies, and live organisms.

JUST LINERS, INC.
P. O. Box 79
Bogota, TN 38007
888/838-4017
www.justliners.com
Equipment—not just liners.

WATER GARDEN GEMS, INC.
3136 Bolton Rd.
Marion, TX 78124
800/682-6098
www.watergardengems.com
Equipment and some plants.

Fish

DRS. FOSTER AND SMITH
2253 Air Park Rd.
Rhinelander, WI 54501
800/381-7179
www.drsfostersmith.com
Order on-line or from catalog. Fish, plants, equipment, and supplies.

Membership organizations

ASSOCIATED KOI CLUBS OF AMERICA
P.O. Box 469070
Escondido, CA 92046
888/660-2073
www.akca.org
Membership includes *Koi USA* magazine.

INTERNATIONAL WATER LILY AND WATER GARDENING SOCIETY
6828 26th St. W
Bradenton, FL 34207
941/756-0880
email:info@iwgs.org
www.iwgs.org
Membership includes *Water Garden Journal*. Website includes a comprehensive directory of resources, including retail, wholesale, mail-order, Internet, manufacturers, growers, designers, installers, distributors, and publishers.

NORTH AMERICAN WATER GARDEN SOCIETY (NAWGS)
630/326-1726
www.nawgs.com
An organization of pond lovers dedicated to enjoyment, education, promotion, and preservation of the water garden hobby. Membership includes subscription to *Aquascape LifeStyles* magazine.

Miscellaneous

AVIAN AQUATICS, INC.
P.O. Box 295
Nassau, DE 19969
800/788-6478
www.avianaquatics.com
Water features for songbirds.

Plants

GREEN & HAGSTROM, INC.
7767 Fernvale Rd.
Fairview, TN 37062
615/799-0708
www.greenandhagstrom.com
Plants and fish; also equipment.

MARYLAND AQUATIC NURSERIES, INC.
3427 N. Furnace Rd.
Jarrettsville, MD 21084
410/557-7615
www.marylandaquatic.com
Plants, equipment, fountains for indoors and out.

PERRY'S WATER GARDENS
136 Gibson Aquatic Farm Rd.
Franklin, NC 28734
828/524-3264
Plants.

SLOCUM WATER GARDENS
P.O. Box 7079
Winter Haven, FL 33883
863/293-7151
Plants, goldfish, koi, and equipment.

WILDLIFE NURSERIES, INC.
P.O. Box 2724
Oshkosh, WI 54903-2724
920/231-3780
Hardy perennial aquatic, and wetland plants, available in quantities of 1–1,000 stems.

WILLIAM TRICKER, INC.
7125 Tanglewood Dr.
Independence, OH 44131
800/524-3492
www.tricker.com
Plants and equipment.

Publications

***WATER GARDENING* MAGAZINE**
P.O. Box 607
St. John, IN 46373
Ph: 800/308-6157
www.watergardening.com

INDEX

Page numbers in **bold type** indicate Gallery entries and always include photographs. Page numbers in *italic type* indicate additional photographs. All plants are listed under their common names.

USDA PLANT HARDINESS ZONE MAP

This map of climate zones helps you select plants for your garden that will survive a typical winter in your region. The United States Department of Agriculture (USDA) developed the map, basing the zones on the lowest recorded temperatures across North America. Zone 1 is the coldest area and Zone 11 is the warmest.

Plants are classified by the coldest temperature and zone they can endure. For example, plants hardy to Zone 6 survive where winter temperatures drop to –10° F. Those hardy to Zone 8 die long before it's that cold. These plants may grow in colder regions but must be replaced each year. Plants rated for a range of hardiness zones can usually survive winter in the coldest region as well as tolerate the summer heat of the warmest one.

To find your hardiness zone, note the approximate location of your community on the map, then match the color band marking that area to the key.

HAWAII

AUSTRALIA

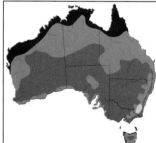

UNITED KINGDOM

Range of Average Annual Minimum Temperatures for Each Zone

- Zone 1: Below -50° F (below -45.6° C)
- Zone 2: -50 to -40° F (-45.5 to -40° C)
- Zone 3: -40 to -30° F (-39.9 to -34.5° C)
- Zone 4: -30 to -20° F (-34.4 to -28.9° C)
- Zone 5: -20 to -10° F (-28.8 to -23.4° C)
- Zone 6: -10 to 0° F (-23.3 to -17.8° C)
- Zone 7: 0 to 10° F (-17.7 to -12.3° C)
- Zone 8: 10 to 20° F (-12.2 to -6.7° C)
- Zone 9: 20 to 30° F (-6.6 to -1.2° C)
- Zone 10: 30 to 40° F (-1.1 to 4.4° C)
- Zone 11: Above 40° F (above 4.5° C)

AMERICAN HORTICULTURAL SOCIETY PLANT HEAT ZONE MAP

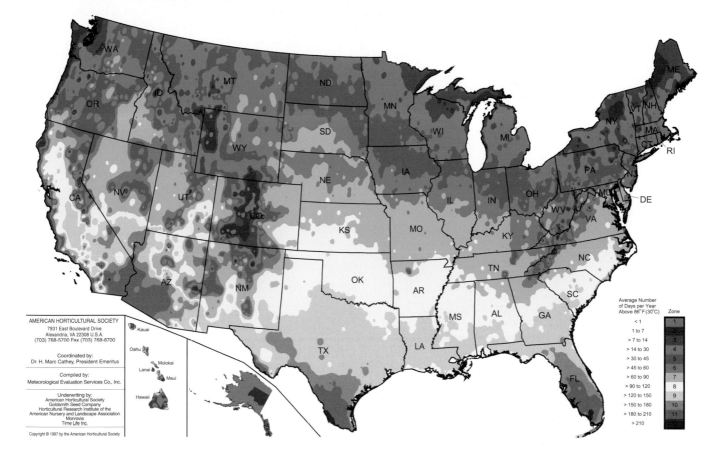

AMERICAN HORTICULTURAL SOCIETY
7931 East Boulevard Drive
Alexandria, VA 22308 U.S.A.
(703) 768-5700 Fax (703) 768-8700

Coordinated by:
Dr. H. Marc Cathey, President Emeritus

Compiled by:
Meteorological Evaluation Services Co., Inc.

Underwriting by:
American Horticultural Society
Goldsmith Seed Company
Horticultural Research Institute of the
American Nursery and Landscape Association
Monrovia
Time Life Inc.

Copyright © 1997 by the American Horticultural Society

Average Number of Days per Year Above 86°F (30°C) — **Zone**

Days	Zone
< 1	1
1 to 7	2
> 7 to 14	3
> 14 to 30	4
> 30 to 45	5
> 45 to 60	6
> 60 to 90	7
> 90 to 120	8
> 120 to 150	9
> 150 to 180	10
> 180 to 210	11
> 210	12

METRIC CONVERSIONS

U.S. Units to Metric Equivalents			Metric Units to U.S. Equivalents		
To Convert From	**Multiply By**	**To Get**	**To Convert From**	**Multiply By**	**To Get**
Inches	25.4	Millimeters	Millimeters	0.0394	Inches
Inches	2.54	Centimeters	Centimeters	0.3937	Inches
Feet	30.48	Centimeters	Centimeters	0.0328	Feet
Feet	0.3048	Meters	Meters	3.2808	Feet
Yards	0.9144	Meters	Meters	1.0936	Yards
Square inches	6.4516	Square centimeters	Square centimeters	0.1550	Square inches
Square feet	0.0929	Square meters	Square meters	10.764	Square feet
Square yards	0.8361	Square meters	Square meters	1.1960	Square yards
Acres	0.4047	Hectares	Hectares	2.4711	Acres
Cubic inches	16.387	Cubic centimeters	Cubic centimeters	0.0610	Cubic inches
Cubic feet	0.0283	Cubic meters	Cubic meters	35.315	Cubic feet
Cubic feet	28.316	Liters	Liters	0.0353	Cubic feet
Cubic yards	0.7646	Cubic meters	Cubic meters	1.308	Cubic yards
Cubic yards	764.55	Liters	Liters	0.0013	Cubic yards

To convert from degrees Fahrenheit (F) to degrees Celsius (C), first subtract 32, then multiply by ⁵⁄₉.

To convert from degrees Celsius to degrees Fahrenheit, multiply by ⁹⁄₅, then add 32.